# BEYOND
## THE
# SUBCONSCIOUS
## The Ultimate Mind Game

Chuck Francis

Library of Congress Catalog No. 88-081688
ISBN No. 0-9620761-0-4

This book is dedicated to the most important person in the world...

- The Seeker of Truth...

- The One Who is Tired of Being Flim-Flammed, Mis-Guided, Misinformed and Generally Ripped Off...

- The Individual Who is Now Ready to be Freed From the Bonds of Ignorance.

# TABLE OF CONTENTS

# PART TWO

## Techniques And Tools

Hello! My name is Chuck Francis.

I realize this is a rather unorthodox way of introducing a book; however, I've been doing things in unusual and unexpected ways for many years and I don't intend to stop now. You see, by going beyond the ordinary; by probing deeper into things that might seem trivial to others, I've discovered some astounding facts that thousands of writers, philosophers, theologians, teachers and other learned mortals have overlooked in their search for the ultimate truth.

I've attempted, over the years, to pass on my discoveries to anyone who would listen. Unfortunately, most people couldn't grasp the meaning of what I was saying. As a result, I was often ridiculed; however, I believed I was right. I decided, therefore, that the most effective way of communicating to others and share my secrets was to write a book. "Beyond The Subconscious" is the result. I didn't write it because I wanted to—but because I had to.

During my search for the truth, I spent a small fortune on all types of motivational programs. You name it—I bought it. I soon realized I was merely making others rich. By a divine stroke of providence, I discovered the "real truth" on my own in 1975. I made a promise, right then and there, that when I found myself in the position to write a book explaining the "SECRET," I would do so. In this manner, I realized everyone could see the real truth and enjoy success and happiness. "Beyond The Subconscious" is the fulfillment of my wish; the answer to my dreams.

The methods and techniques I've used over the years have worked for me without fail. I've attained financial independence, so money is the least of my worries. I have also obtained more important things, like peace of mind and a deep spiritual understanding. I turned my life around 180° and you can do the same by following the methods and techniques outlined in the book. Success can be yours beyond your wildest dreams. The information contained in "Beyond The Subconscious" can make it happen. It's the "Ultimate Mind Game."

—Chuck Francis

# PART ONE

# CHAPTER ONE

# IN SEARCH
# OF THE
# TRUTH

*"The Longest Journey
Begins With
The First Step."*

27

_____*THE SEARCH BEGINS*

In our search for the truth we travel many roads, most of which end in a maze of confusion and misunderstanding. Most of us depend on others to show us the way, to carve paths through the jungles of ignorance. We are taught to be followers, not leaders, and to accept what is given to us. I was no exception. Like millions of others, I wasted a good part of my life in the belief that wealth, happiness and success were reserved, in some mysterious way, for a select few and that I was destined to sit back and be content with "just getting by." I accepted the premise that my environment dictated my future and there was no way to escape. Words like "Stay in your place" and "You'll never amount to anything" still echo in my ears and I know that the very same words are being spoken today to millions who believe, as I did, that the future holds little promise for them. It's unfortunate, but true. The majority of people in the world are confined within the small society into which they were born. It's as if there is a barrier surrounding them and they are convinced, just as I once was, that there is "no way out." The truth is, there is a way out. The powerful, yet simple, secret is hidden in a place that remains virtually unexplored.

## _____WASTED YEARS

Looking back, I realize that most of my early life was a one-way street to oblivion. It had been virtually wasted. As a child I had been taught to stay within the limits of my own society; to be forever trapped within the mold that cast me. As a result I had acquired the Midas touch in reverse. Almost everything I did was wrong. I couldn't find a mate; I felt inferior to others and had almost no friends. It was at this point in my life that I decided to escape from my world of misery and poverty.

## _____THE SEARCH THAT LED NOWHERE

In an attempt to find happiness and success I turned to outside sources for guidance. I read countless "positive thinking" type books; attended seminars and listened to dozens of tapes, but they didn't work. I even tried those "subliminal message" tapes, thinking perhaps they held some sort of hidden messages that would penetrate my subconscious mind and "plant" the seeds of success. While interesting, to a degree, I finally realized they weren't for me. I didn't know exactly why at the time but the answer came to me later. The subliminal messages were not of MY doing, but someone else's. THEY were claiming to plant ideas in my mind when I was the one who should have been in control and planted them myself. It's much like planting a garden. Unless you, yourself, plant the seeds in your garden, you will never know what was planted for sure until it matures. The same principle holds true, I was to later discover, with our individual desires.

We, ourselves, must plant the subliminal seeds of success. In this way, we can be sure our efforts will result in harvesting a bumper crop. Therefore, in my case, someone else's subliminal motivational tapes proved to be an expensive wasted experiment. I just got deeper into debt and was more confused than ever.

After the books, seminars and tapes proved useless, my search for the truth turned to simple prayer. Even praying didn't help. Perhaps I didn't know how at the time.

Frankly, I couldn't understand where I had gone wrong. Why had a lot of people with whom I had gone to school become so successful? Why did they always have such good grades and find great jobs when they graduated? Why had they found spouses so quickly and settled down to "live happily ever after?" Why?

## A HOPELESS SITUATION

Things reached a point where I started to apologize for living. Then things got worse. I hit absolute rock-bottom in 1975. In my search for success I had moved to Phoenix, Arizona in 1973. The recession set in a year later and the local unemployment rate skyrocketed to a whopping 17%. The economy was so bad that when I went to the unemployment office, I had to park almost a quarter of a mile away. I couldn't even get a job washing dishes.

## UNREAL ESTATE

A few months earlier I had tried my hand at real estate on a commission basis but that, too, proved fruitless. In fact, the realtors I worked for were in a financial bind themselves. They even offered to sell me a house they owned with no money down if I could make the payments. (Little did I know at the time that I would soon own the house because I was on the verge of discovering the SECRET that would turn my life around!)

All I had was a lonely apartment and the rent was overdue. Night after night I sat there, alone, broke and friendless. It was the darkest time of my entire life. It seemed as though I was trapped in a corner from which there was no escape. But was there?

_____THE SECRET IS DISCOVERED

I'll never forget the moment it happened. I had just gone to bed and was almost asleep, more or less in a "limbo state" of semi-sleep, when, like a blinding light, the "secret" made itself known to me! An exhilarating sensation of pins and needles raced up and down my spine in an overwhelming surge of happiness. In one split second I **KNEW THE SECRET OF SUCCESS!** The secret had been in front of me all my life but I had been too confused to see it. From that moment on I have had nothing but prosperity and peace of mind.

**Without being fully aware of it, I had bypassed my conscious and subconscious mind and discovered a powerful force within me that I had communicated with through my IMAGINATION!**

_____*THE VOW*

The secret proved to be so simple that I said to myself it couldn't be true; yet I knew deep down in my heart that it was. I absolutely KNEW things were going to change for the better. Right at that "moment of truth," I made this vow:

> WHEN THE TIME CAME THAT I WOULD BE ABLE TO SHARE THIS GREAT TRUTH WITH OTHERS, I WOULD DO SO.

Now is that time! The secret is contained time and time again within the pages of this book and the methods and techniques of using this secret to its fullest potential are the ones I have used over the years. You possess the secret right at this moment. The powerful force that will give you any reasonable thing you want is within you and you can use it to turn desires into reality and make your dreams come true.

_____*PUTTING THE SECRET TO WORK*

It wasn't long after I discovered this great truth that my new knowledge was put to the test. One day I opened the door to my apartment only to find the landlord standing there with an eviction notice in his hand. A thought raced through my mind. Would the secret REALLY work? As my hand reached for the eviction notice my heart pounded and the "pins and needles" sensation raced through my body just as it did when I first discovered the true secret. Now I knew it was working!

The landlord didn't know that a few days earlier the real estate company I had worked for offered to sell me a house they owned for the payments only. In fact, I had imagined owning a house only a few weeks earlier. I took the eviction notice from the landlord and thanked him. Within minutes the phone rang and the initial payment for the house was granted me almost like magic from a private source. It was the break I needed and I KNOW it happened because the force I discovered within me MADE it happen. (And it can do the same for you!)

Shortly after moving into my newly acquired house, someone gave me a good job. That sounds pretty normal—except for one thing—I hadn't even applied for it. Remember, the unemployment rate was still 17%. Not bad for a new beginning, was it?

Now, it's my sincere desire that you, too, from this day forward, will become the person you want to be and get the things you deserve in life.

_____*THE SECRET*

I'm sure by now that you want to know exactly just what WAS the secret I discovered on that lonely night in 1975. Before you use the methods and techniques in the book, it is necessary to discuss the secret—or to put it more aptly—the "force" that made itself known to me. As I said before, the secret is so simple it's hard to believe, yet it's true.

I realized, soon after my initial experience, that I received the true secret from the Higher Force that resides in all of us. I knew it was not from my conscious or subconscious mind because I had gone that route before via the subliminal tapes, seminars, books, etc. The secret had to come from beyond the subconscious. The fact that I had been backed into a corner, with no place to go, convinced me that the answer to life's mysteries was within my Spiritual Self.

## THE NEW BEGINNING

I knew my search for the truth had finally come to a new beginning that fateful night in 1975. Upon reflection, I have to smile when I remember the diverse routes I travelled during the search. My journey was so intense and thorough that I looked for magic potions, special incantations to see the "light;" secret books, a guru, a yogi—even the high lama. I had thought, perhaps, it might be possible that some mighty person held this valuable information, this truth in trust, guarding it for humanity at large. As stated previously, I turned to religion with a fervor and visited the major churches of the world hoping I could find the answers to my many questions. All I did was come away with more questions than answers. Please be assured I am not putting down any religion. Far from it. If one believes in a certain religion, then this, indeed, is good.

## YOU CAN'T TAKE IT WITH YOU (OR CAN YOU?)

The majority of people in the world today accept the fact that we shed our physical body when we leave the Earth. In spite of this, there are still many civilizations that hold onto the notion that physical possessions accompany us during our journey into the "great beyond." Ancient Egyptians, Early American Indians and the Incas are prime examples of civilizations that held this belief for centuries. In addition, these people placed their faith and belief in physical objects.

We, in our complacency, might look at these people as naive and even ignorant. Yet we, ourselves, are engulfed in a sea of superstition that is nothing short of staggering. During my search for the "true secret," I visited many libraries and uncovered a vast storehouse of ancient beliefs and customs which we carry on today! I discovered literally thousands of them and all are connected, in one way or another, with fear of the "unknown" manifested through physical objects. Perhaps we don't fully realize it, but we are actually imparting "magical powers" to them, as if the "Higher Force" dwells within them, controlling our destinies. The truth is, the Higher Force can be found only within our Spiritual Selves.

Why, then, do we continue to treat physical objects as possessing some mysterious power? Because, deep down in our hearts, we carry on the ancient traditions of our ancestors and refuse to admit that the "true force" always has been, and always will be, within us. What we should be doing is taking a good look at our Spiritual Self because that's where we'll find the true power. We are the temple in which the Higher Force resides, waiting to do our bidding. It, and it alone, will survive forever. CONCLUSION: Just as we cannot take our physical possessions with us when we leave Earth, neither can we take the physical objects in which we placed our faith. Therefore, **DOES IT MAKE ANY SENSE TO EVEN**

**BOTHER WITH THEM TO BEGIN WITH?** What do you think? . . .

I realized, many years ago, that I could "clothe" the true secret in some mysterious form; to make it some sort of "magical formula" available to only a fortunate few. But I preferred, if given the chance, to put it right out in the open and the information in this book does it the best way I know how. After all, why hide the very thing that could take mankind out of the dark ages? Perhaps I just got "lucky" when I found out that the "true secret," the truth of mankind, had been buried within me all my life!

### —————————TAP INTO YOUR SPIRITUAL SELF

Once you have discovered the purity and simplicity of the methods and techniques outlined in this book, you will be able to tap into your Spiritual Self and you will see signs everywhere in which direction to go to put your newly found inner strength to good use. **THIS INFORMATION AND KNOWLEDGE YOU CAN TAKE WITH YOU—BECAUSE IT IS ETERNAL.** Think about it. When you shed your Physical body, this information still resides within you and it cannot be taken from you by anyone! It's yours to use FOREVER. The miracle of life is within you; this is the ultimate answer.

### —————————————PLACING THE BLAME

After I discovered the "Great Truth," it wasn't long before I realized what I had been doing a good part of my life—

blaming my misfortune and my failures on others plus my environment. In truth, I had been trapped by my own past and rather than trying to escape from it, I dwelled in my own misery. **It was I, and I alone,** who was responsible for my failures and it was up to me to change my attitude; to stop feeling sorry for myself. Since I had worked so hard to create my failures, I knew I had to change my way of thinking and reverse the self-destruction process. By thinking NEGATIVELY I had created NEGATIVE RESULTS. Therefore, it made sense to turn this process AROUND and allow my Imagination to work FOR me instead of AGAINST me. Everything I needed for success, happiness and peace of mind was contained within me (you too). All I had to do was direct the Higher Force, this awesome power, to give me the things I wanted. You might call this "force" by another name: "God"—The "Inner Mind"—The "Spirit"—or whatever you wish. In any case, you can be sure it's there. The methods and techniques that follow in this book will show you how to go beyond your subconscious and put this awe-inspiring force to work for you.

## _____HOW THE SECRET WORKS

So far, I've explained the basic secret in its Spiritual form. There is also a "mental" aspect to the secret that you should know at this point before delving into the methods and techniques. This element is vitally important to understand before continuing. Therefore, I will briefly explain it now so you will be prepared to put it to use later on:

## "EVERYTHING MAN-MADE WAS FIRST A THOUGHT AND THEN A THING."

To demonstrate this, look at the book you are now reading. Before it was printed it was first a thought. Only by "seeing" this book through my imagination first was I able to make it a reality. This simple, yet powerful concept holds true with any reasonable thing you want! Remember these important words:

## "YOU MUST FIRST IMAGINE WHAT YOU WANT AND KNOW THAT IT ALREADY EXISTS—AND YOU WILL RECEIVE IT!"

If you do this, you WILL get the things you want. After all, I imagined nothing but misery and poverty for many years and that's exactly what I got—misery and poverty.

## "YOU ARE TODAY WHO YOU THOUGHT YOU WERE YESTERDAY"

_____IT'S TIME TO TURN YOUR LIFE AROUND

By following the techniques closely and giving yourself reasonable desires and a reasonable amount of time to achieve them, you will turn your life around in a fashion so dramatic you won't believe it happened. They produced many riches for me, especially peace of mind which is so important to all of us.

You'll discover the information is easy to follow. I've attempted to strip away the mountain of oratory and misinformation contained in so-called "self-improvement" programs that, instead of revealing the secrets of success, actually hide them.

By now I suppose you realize that it's my sincere desire to see you prosper. Obviously, I haven't had the opportunity to explain all the various facets of the "Great Truth" in this first chapter. As you read further, more aspects of it will become clear to you. Let it suffice to say that a powerful force lies within you, waiting to do your bidding—RIGHT NOW.

_____SUMMATION

1. The secret of happiness and success is hidden in a place that remains virtually unexplored.

2. Plant the seeds of success yourself—not by others. In this way you can be assured of a bumper crop.

3. Don't allow your environment to dictate your future.

4. When you discover the secret of success you will feel a "pins and needles" sensation within you.

5. You must go beyond the subconscious to discover the awesome power—the Higher Force that dwells within you.

6. You must reverse negative attitudes and turn them into positive ones.

7. Everything man-made was first a thought and then a thing.

8. You must first imagine what you want and know that it already exists and you will receive it.

9. You are today who you thought you were yesterday.

# CHAPTER TWO

# UNDERSTANDING

# YOURSELF

*"We Are Spiritual Beings
Pretending To Be
Physical Beings."*

_____*THE THREE OF YOU*

Before you even begin to think about who you want to be in life and the things you desire, it's of the utmost importance that you understand yourself.

After inhabiting the world for millions of years, mankind has come to the conclusion that we are the highest form of life on the planet Earth; a tri-level entity composed of the following parts:

•

PHYSICAL

•

MENTAL

•

SPIRITUAL

_____THE "I AM"

All three parts are inter-connected and controlled by the "I AM," or conscious part of the being. The "I AM" can dwell in one or all parts at the same time:

PHYSICAL

MENTAL

SPIRITUAL

First is the Physical. Beyond the Physical lies the Mental and beyond the Mental lies the Spiritual.
Within the Spiritual is a powerful force waiting to do our bidding. In order to make this force work for you, it's necessary to understand the three parts of yourself.

_____PHYSICAL

Lifespan: 0-120 years or more.
Composition: Trillions of atoms

The Physical body is constantly rebuilding itself, shedding cells and growing new ones; replenishing energy and healing wounds.
It's estimated that the body completely rebuilds itself every six months.

In spite of the wonders contained in our bodies, we know the Physical part is temporary—and that's the way it must be. The Physical body is merely the storehouse for our Mental and Spiritual selves. However, our Physical body is a demanding machine that must be controlled, otherwise it will control us. We all know the problems it presents to us. If we feed ourselves the wrong foods, or too much food, we will become fat and sluggish. If we force smoke into our lungs, we can expect the consequences. If we abuse our body, odds are we shall die young. We all know these things, yet too many of us continue to ignore the warnings and become one-sided. We fail to recognize the great wonders of the world that abound all around us. We become trapped in our one-sided world and accept our failures. As a result we are forced to "live on the outside, looking in."

How do we know when the Physical part of a human being is in control? The signs are endless:

• You find yourself lying, cheating or stealing.

• You feel helpless, as if there's no hope.

• You feel inferior to others, as though everyone is "better than you."

• You accept the idea that you must live in poverty.

• You allow your sex drive to rule your life.

• You become envious and jealous of others.

• You become greedy and grasping.

• You let money become your god.

• You develop many phobias.

• You step on others to get ahead.

- In general, you have little compassion for any living thing.

The list could go on and on.

It's sad but true that more and more people today allow only the Physical part to control their lives. They feed their bodies with harmful substances such as drugs, junk food, alcohol, tobacco, etc.

When the Physical part is allowed to take control, the Mental and Spiritual parts are suppressed, unable to contribute, thereby making you an incomplete person. The only way you can change this is for you to control the Physical instead of letting it control you. Remember, it's the only part of a human being that will not survive forever, so TAKE CARE OF IT!

_____MENTAL

### Lifespan: Infinite

The Mental part of a human being is known by various names: The Brain. The Conscious Mind. The Subconscious Mind, etc. It's important to realize, however, that the brain itself is not the actual Mental part, but rather the link between the Physical and Spiritual. It collects uncountable bits of information during one's lifetime, yet we will probably never know its full potential. In spite of its complexity, science has determined many of its capabilities. They are, indeed, astounding. For example, the memory center, located within the brain, can store up to 500 times more information than a full set of the most comprehensive encyclopaedia. Expressed another way, the brain contains more information than all the greatest libraries of the world. Weighing approximately three pounds, it can perform the same amount of functions of a computer the combined size of Ohio, Indiana and Kentucky, assuming such a computer could be built. Composed of literally billions of nerve cells, the brain can store 280 Quintillion bits of information. Perhaps, someday, science will fathom the brain's full capabilities and unravel the mysteries surrounding it.

_____THE MENTAL "I AM"

As stated previously, the "I AM" can dwell in the Mental part of a human being just as it can dwell in and control the Physical and Spiritual parts. You can tell the Mental "I AM" is in control when you start applying "logic" and "limitations" to your thoughts and deeds. We've been drawing false conclusions since the beginning of civilization, only to find out later that our Mental Self limited, and even blotted out, our ultimate capabilities. We're all familiar with some of these past conclusions that later proved to be false, simply because we allowed the Mental to take control:

• The Earth is flat.

• Man will never reach the Moon.

• A human can't run a 4-minute mile.

• Rome will never fall.

• Man cannot fly.

• If man goes into space, the world shall be destroyed.

- Hard work makes you rich.
- Matter cannot travel faster than the speed of light.
- It's impossible to remember the future.
- The Titanic is unsinkable.
- Nice guys finish last.
- It's aerodynamically impossible for bumblebees to fly.
- Mt. Everest is unconquerable.
- An airplane can never break the sound barrier.
- No one will ever break Babe Ruth's home run record.
- The automobile will never replace the horse and buggy.
- It's impossible for human beings to travel faster than 20 mph; otherwise, they will smother to death.
- Portable radios can't be made.
- Chuck Francis will never amount to anything.
- The atom cannot be split.
- Tomatoes are poisonous.
- No one will ever break Ty Cobb's record for hits.
- No one can live with an artificial heart.
- Elvis Presley will never be popular. The Beatles won't either.
- The typewriter will never replace a good clerk.
- The telephone is just "an electrical toy" and nothing else.
- I'll never get what I want or become the person I want to be.
- Success and happiness are reserved for only a select few.

These are just a few examples of our thinking when it comes from the Mental Self, whether it be from the conscious or subconscious. It's only when we allow our "I AM" to dwell within our Spiritual Self that we are able to do the "impossible."

_____*SPIRITUAL*

### Lifespan: Eternal

We have been attempting to define our Spiritual Self ever since our ancestors carved crude symbols on the walls of their caves. All of us, at some point in our lives, become acutely aware of our Spiritual Self. Both our Physical and Mental parts are rather easily discernible as we have discussed. We can see and feel our body; we can think rationally and control our mind. Yet, when we come to the Spiritual part of ourselves, we become confused. Some of us even deny it exists and continue to use only two parts of our being. We eat. We sleep. We work. We entertain our minds and bodies. When we attempt to enter the Spiritual part of ourself, we hesitate. Some of us put our faith in physical objects just as ancient Egyptians did when they adored the Sun god Ra. Some people give magical powers to amulets, crystals—even rabbits' feet. The truth is, it's our Spiritual Self that opens the door to the "magical power" that makes our dreams come true. The problem we have with our Spiritual Self is that it cannot be seen or touched. The most eloquent poet cannot begin to describe it, although many have tried. **The Spiritual Self can only be experienced!**

Since we, as humans, are limited in our capacity to

fully understand our existence, we must rely on what we experience. We know what "hot and cold" means; we know the physical and mental pangs of hunger; the joys of love and the physical and mental comforts of a home and family. At the same time we practically hide our Spiritual Self under a blanket of confusion . . . and, perhaps, fear. In truth, communicating with the Higher Force within your Spiritual Self through your Imagination is an experience you'll never forget. All you have to do is allow it to happen. It's not reserved for "special" people and once you have accomplished it and understand the "who, what and where," nothing will be able to hold you back from achieving your desires. Perhaps you've been led to believe that communicating with this power is difficult. Actually, it's one of the easiest things to do and it's accomplished by going beyond the subconscious.

## A POWERFUL FORCE IS WAITING TO BE SUMMONED

Within your Spiritual Self lies the most powerful force in existence. It can truly move mountains and it is, at this very moment, residing within you, begging to be summoned!

Exactly, then, what is this power? Is it the Soul? Is it really "God"—the Fourth Dimension—The "Boss?" Is it Einstein's "X"? Actually, it's all of these—or none of these—because it doesn't matter what you call it, as long as you are aware of its existence.

For the sake of argument and convenience, let us say this power resides beyond the conscious and subconscious

and it can be activated through that part of us we call the
IMAGINATION.

We all allow our imaginations to run wild. We all
derive pleasure from "imagining" things we don't have: a
new car, fancy home, a yacht, fantastic health and peace of
mind, to name just a few. Yet, if we can focus our
thoughts on just a select few desires through our imagination, much like we focus the Sun's rays through a magnify-
ing glass, then those things we imagine will become
realities.

_____WHAT YOU REALLY ARE

You must realize that you are a Spiritual Being pretending to be a Physical Being. Remember, the Physical is
temporary, the Mental is a storehouse of facts, figures and
memory, and the Spiritual is eternal. This is why the
Spiritual Self houses the ultimate power. Think about it.
The Physical can only react in a physical manner. The
Mental can control the Physical but is limited in its
capabilities. It takes, therefore, something far more
powerful to bring about the dramatic results we desire
and this power can only come by going beyond the subconscious through our Imagination.

_____LET THE "I AM" DWELL IN THE SPIRITUAL

Previously, I discussed some examples of our thinking
when we allow the Physical and Mental parts to take
control. Once you allow the "I AM" to dwell in the

Spiritual Self, your thoughts and attitudes will automatically change from negative to positive. Here are a few examples:

- All people are good.
- Evil does not exist.
- I love all people and all things.
- I feel that nothing is impossible.
- I want to help all mankind.
- I feel the "pins and needles" sensation of happiness and fulfillment.
- I know no anger.
- Everything is one.
- To cheat, steal or do wrong, or take from another human being, is the same as doing these things to one's own self.

_____*SUMMATION*

1. You are a Spiritual Being pretending to be a Physical Being.

2. Treat your Spiritual, Mental and Physical selves with the utmost care.

3. The three parts of a human being—Physical, Mental and Spiritual—are linked in a cycle, an unbroken circle; each being part of the other, each being part of the whole.

4. The Mental controls the Physical; the Spiritual controls the Mental; all three control each other.

5. Call upon the Higher Force within you to give you the things you want and not only will you receive them but you will benefit everyone and everything around you.

# WHAT MAKES YOU SUCCESSFUL?

*"You Never Fail
Until You
Stop Trying."*

57

_THE TRUE MEANING_

Success is a state of mind. No one can tell you whether you are successful or not. Only you know.

IF YOU FEEL SUCCESSFUL, YOU ARE SUCCESSFUL.

This may seem, at first glance, an over-simplification. It's true, however, because success isn't what you might think. It isn't money, friends, appearance or anything physical. **Success is a feeling produced when one's life is in order.**

When the majority of things fall into place the way you want them to, then you can consider yourself as being successful. You should never be misled into assuming that success is measured by material possessions. History constantly reminds us of this fact. So many people have attempted to use money as a yardstick but their tragic lives proved otherwise. In spite of this, money continues to be a top priority. This doesn't mean, of course, that you should subject yourself to a life of poverty and its accompanying misery. Far from it! You can still have a million dollars in the bank; a Lincoln Town Car; a yacht; a beautiful family and a close circle of friends. However, if your life is not in order; if you don't have true peace of mind regarding your existence on Earth, then success will continue to elude you.

## HOW TO ATTAIN SUCCESS

How, then, can you attain the feeling of success? As stated earlier, "When you feel successful, you **are** successful." This will be an automatic feeling with no conscious effort on your part—once you have mastered the simple techniques in this book. Already, without practicing them as yet, you should have a certain feeling of contentment and relaxation; a sense of trust and well-being; a belief in your own capabilities and talents. Soon, with practice, you will be in the proper state of mind.

Success is the result of accomplishing a goal; attaining a wish. It's like putting the final piece of a jigsaw puzzle into place. The enjoyment you get is not the final completed picture, but rather the challenge that was presented to you. Indeed, once the puzzle is completed the joy is over and you seek another puzzle to solve. It's not really the goal that matters; it's the thrill and the feeling of reaching it that counts. It's the excitement of overcoming hardships that stand in your way before you finally accomplish what you set out to do.

## GETTING WHAT YOU DESIRE

It doesn't make any difference what you desire, as long as it's within reason for you and you set a reasonable amount of time to achieve it. You might want to attract money; lose weight; stop smoking; locate your perfect mate; get a good job; increase sales; be your own boss; get better grades—or to just feel happier. True success is everything leading to what you desire, giving your life meaning and direction. Success is always having another desire in mind. This way you can avoid the "let down" feeling that inevitably follows the completion of a goal. This is so true in everyday life.

Most every teenager in America knows what a thrill it is to own that "first car." It's a special car; a beautiful piece of machinery eager to take its proud owner anyplace. The first day the owner sits behind the wheel is a very happy one. The second day is still a happy occasion and the pride of ownership continues throughout the week. A month passes and the car gradually loses some of its lustre. Perhaps the carburetor acts up and funny noises come from the hood. Before you know it, the teenager is looking for another car; a better one. And so it is with practically everything in life. We must constantly have new desires; find new horizons and not be content to sit back and let the world go by.

## OVERNIGHT SUCCESS

Don't be misled into thinking that success can be yours within 24 hours, or even 24 days. In real life there is no such thing as an "overnight success story." Every meaningful event in life is the result of careful planning; every successful person is the result of patience coupled with positive action.

Far too many of us have stars in our eyes, expecting good things to come to us without much effort on our part. We look for magic pills, the "quick fix," the Fountain of Youth and countless other "miracles" that will come our way. We constantly peer into a sea of darkness and wait for our "ship to come in." What we SHOULD be doing is building that ship and then setting out from shore on our journey of life. We should be forging the steel, cutting the trees and sewing the sails of our ship and then, and then only, dare we challenge the world and search for its treasures.

_____*DO IT YOURSELF*

Positive thinking is one thing; positive action is another. You can attend all the seminars you wish; read all the lengthy manuals you can get your hands on; listen to boring subliminal tapes until doomsday and you'll still probably find yourself a confused and unsuccessful person searching for true success. Why? As stated earlier in this book, you are following someone else's advice and persuasion—NOT YOUR OWN! Remember, the secret of success is within YOU and only you and it's up to you to bring it out.

_____*MAKING OTHERS RICH*

When you rely on other people's philosophies for success and happiness and purchase their "wares", you are contributing to their bank accounts, not yours. You might say,

"Well, what is Chuck Francis doing by selling me this book?" To this I say, I'm really not concerned about making money. Chances are, I'll lose a great deal financially, since it's extremely expensive to publish a book of this magnitude and nature and have it become a bestseller. But what I lose financially I will gain spiritually. If only one person, perhaps yourself, gains a little insight into the true meaning of your life, then I will consider myself wealthy beyond description. You see, I wrote this book **AFTER** I acquired my material possessions. To my knowledge, most of the other so-called self-improvement programs, books and tapes are written by people who make these vehicles their prime source of income. I proved to **myself** first that my methods would work **before** I sat down to write "Beyond The Subconscious." In this way, I **KNOW** the methods and techniques will work for others, just as they did, and continue to do so, for me. Perhaps I didn't have to include this section in the book, but my conscience wouldn't allow me to rest if I omitted it. In any event, I want to assure you that by "doing it yourself" you are creating your own success story and not depending on someone else to lead you by the hand. The "true secret" lies within you; a powerful force only you can summon. You are the master of your destiny. This book merely points the way.

_____*SETTING THE STAGE FOR SUCCESS*

Perhaps the great dancer, Fred Astaire, is the perfect example of what I mean by "positive action," as mentioned previously. His seemingly effortless dancing on the screen was the result of countless hours, days and months of rehearsal. It's said that just thirty seconds of one of his dancing scenes took up to thirty hours of practice and he didn't stop until the sequence was flawless.

We can set our own stage for success with positive action, too, by DOING and not WISHING. How often do you say, "I wish I had this . . . I wish I could do that?" What you should be saying is, "I'm going to have this . . . I'm going to do that!" Then you prepare yourself for it by taking positive action. So many of us "wish upon a star," then crawl back into our shells and dream away our lives. By taking positive action in everything we do, true success shall be ours for the asking.

## THE HARDER I WORK THE LUCKIER I GET

The next time you admire (not envy) a successful person, don't assume they got "lucky" and hit it big. You can be sure they devoted their entire energy into their desires and their "overnight success" was due to positive action, not wishful thinking. The Higher Force will give you any reasonable thing you want, but you've got to do your part, too; then, one day, you can look in the mirror and say, "What a lucky person I am!" Even when all else fails; when you just can't seem to do anything right, remember this: Positive Action works!

As a matter of fact, there are times when you can even DEMAND that the Higher Force give you the things you desire! This may sound like a radical departure from what we have been discussing, but it's a fact. After you have set the stage for success and taken Positive

Action to get the things you want, and you still don't receive them, then, in all good faith, you can stand up and say to the Higher Force, "I have done everything possible to receive the things I desire. I am **deserving** of them and I feel that they should be given to me!" You'd be surprised as to how readily the Higher Force responds because you stood up to be counted instead of hanging your head in defeat.

Why **should** you get the things you want? Because you're **supposed** to get them! The problem is, you and I, plus a lot of others, have been led to believe **otherwise** all our lives!

_____SUMMATION

1. Success is a state of mind.
2. If you feel successful, you are successful.
3. Success is a feeling produced when one's life is in order.
4. Success doesn't come overnight.
5. You've got to "do it yourself" and not depend on others to do it for you.

# THE BEST-
# KEPT SECRET
# IN THE WORLD

*"Everything Man-Made
Was First A Thought
And Then A Thing."*

69

## MANKIND'S SEARCH

The words and thoughts in this chapter are probably the most important you will ever read in your search for ultimate success, happiness and peace of mind.

Mankind has searched for the "great secret" ever since the discovery of fire and the invention of the wheel. It was assumed this secret was very complicated and it would eventually be found in some hidden corner of the world engraved upon a golden tablet or some other mystic form. Even today, mankind searches for the secret, little realizing that the true secret of success and accomplishment lies right before our eyes. In simple terms, the best-kept secret in the world is: There is no secret!

## THERE IS NO SECRET

It's absolutely true! Life has no secrets. It's out in the open for all to see. The reason we can't see it is because we are looking for something far more complicated and elusive. Life is simple and easy, once you know where to look.

To discover the true secret all one has to do is look beyond the subconscious and that's precisely the purpose of this book. The thoughts and techniques it contains are the very ones I've used for years. They have never failed me and, if used properly, they will never fail you.

In all frankness, the methods used in "Beyond the Subconscious" are so simple, it may take you several of your own personal experiments before you realize how truly easy they are to master. Be assured, right at this moment, that there is a powerful force within you, waiting to grant your every reasonable desire. It's been with us since the beginning of time and the more we try to understand it, the more confused we become. Scientists have tried; philosophers have tried; alchemists, poets and theologians have attempted to unravel the mystery—but all have failed.

THERE IS ONLY ONE WAY TO REACH THIS POWER AND LET IT WORK FOR YOU AND THAT IS THROUGH YOUR IMAGINATION.

One of the most profound facts about our world is this:

EVERYTHING MAN-MADE WAS FIRST A THOUGHT AND THEN A THING.

Again, this fact is really so simple most people overlook it or never even think about it. Every single thing you see around you that is the result of mankind's ability to manufacture objects out of raw matter first existed in someone's mind as a thought before it became a thing. Rudimentary? Of course! But the truth is, it's the most important element to remember in your search for happiness and peace of mind. You have but a fleeting handful of years to discover it so don't waste a moment more!

## IMAGINE IT AND YOU WILL HAVE IT

These words that you are now reading first existed in my Imagination. It would be impossible for me, or anyone else, to sit down at a word processor and automatically type out sensible thoughts and sentences without first using our Imagination. Therefore, since everything was first a thought and then a thing, this book is actually my Imagination manifested in its Physical form!

IT FOLLOWS, THEREFORE, THAT IF YOU IMAGINE SOMETHING YOU REALLY WANT AND IT LIES WITHIN THE REALM OF REASON AND YOU FURTHER IMAGINE IT AS ALREADY BEING YOURS, THEN YOU KNOW IT EXISTS RIGHT NOW AND IT WILL BE GIVEN TO YOU!

## SUBCONSCIOUS INFORMATION AND IMAGINATION INFORMATION

It's important to know the difference between information coming from the subconscious and the information that comes from the Imagination.

Picture, if you will, the subconscious mind as being a complex computer. In spite of its marvels it can only store and impart information fed into it; information that has already come from an original source—the Imagination.

The Imagination gives us information that was never put into it. It creates from scratch. On the other hand, the subconscious can only act when thoughts have been fed into it. The input determines the output. Consider the Imagination as the creator of all man-made things— the originating force that turns thoughts into realities.

## OPENING THE DOOR

The method of imagining something as already being yours, then allowing it to happen, will open the door to success. Imagine what you want and know that it will be yours. If you don't want it, chances are it will never be yours.

It's no secret that all you have to do to get the reasonable things you want is to communicate your desires to the Higher Force through your Imagination, to make your dreams come true!

_____*SUMMATION*

1. The best-kept secret in the world is: There Is No Secret.

2. Everything man-made was first a thought and then a thing.

3. There is only one way to reach the Higher Force within you and that's through your Imagination.

4. You must go beyond the subconscious to unleash the power that is waiting to do your bidding.

5. The subconscious is like a computer that can only impart information fed into it. The input determines the output.

6. The Imagination, starting from scratch, originates the information for the first time and feeds the subconscious.

# CHAPTER FIVE

# OPENING
# THE
# SECRET DOOR

*"A Mental Picture*
*Is Worth More Than*
*A Thousand Words."*

## THE POWER WITHIN

We are all familiar with the word "Imagination" and how much pleasure (or, at times, displeasure) it can give us. I use the word Imagination as a simple, understandable term for the "Secret Door" which leads us beyond the subconscious to the Higher Force.

Many of us remain on a conscious or subconscious level only, without going further; without probing deeper and deeper until we reach this awesome power.

**Within us dwells this power that can and will give us any reasonable thing we want.**

## BEYOND THE SUBCONSCIOUS

Over the years I've developed various methods of using my Imagination. In fact, I constantly develop new ways as I continue to explore this fascinating world within me. Some methods are revealed to me almost by accident. For example, I discovered I can use my Imagination just as easily in a crowd as I can in the solitude of my room. Sometimes it works even better. By and large, however, I give great thought to each method before using it. I make sure it's simple, effective and to the point.

## EXPERIENCING THE
## "PINS AND NEEDLES" SENSATION

Before we discuss some of the various methods of communication, it would be well to further explain the "pins and needles" sensation you will experience when you become aware of the Higher Force within you. As stated in the beginning of this book, I became acutely aware of this sensation in 1975 at the moment I discovered the "secret." This exciting physical sensation will course through your entire body when you realize that the Higher Force within you is ready to do your bidding. At the same moment, a feeling of tranquility and contentment will fill your heart because you absolutely **know** you have finally reached this all-powerful source. To put it another way, it's the PHYSICAL SENSATION YOU EXPERIENCE WHEN YOUR SPIRITUAL SELF IS COMMUNICATING WITH YOU—THE OUTER SELF. The force itself cannot be described—only experienced. You'll know it when it happens.

As far as the PHYSICAL sensation is concerned, it's similar to the feeling you may get when you stand atop a building and peer down at the street below. With most of us, a thrilling "pins and needles" sensation will literally race through our bodies as we recoil from the edge as though a giant, unseen hand is pulling us back to safety. Then, as we gasp for breath, a warm feeling of contentment and tranquility envelops us.

Perhaps you can think of other examples of the "pins and needles" sensation that you have experienced. It might have taken place when you were about to leap from a high diving board into a swimming pool. I can best describe it as that split moment of reality before you act. It's the "moment of truth." (NOTE: It's not necessary to feel the "pins and needles" sensation to realize your desires. Don't worry if you fail to experience it. Some people do—some don't. It will come in due time, automatically. When you imagine the things you desire, they will exist at that moment. Allow them to grow and nurture them with faith and belief and they will come to you with no conscious effort on your part. Be assured that whether you feel the "pins and needles" sensation or not, you can still get the things you want.)

## _YOU CAN'T FOOL YOURSELF

<u>SPECIAL NOTE:</u> Before going into the actual methods, it's important to have a reason for what you desire. It's not good enough to "just want something." You must consider yourself worthy of getting what you are asking for. This is why you must have "reasonable" desires; otherwise, your "belief" will automatically reject them.

Let us suppose your desire is to become a millionaire. Deep down you know you want to "live comfortably" and that you really don't want a "million dollars." So why even ask for it? Therefore, pick the amount of money that seems reasonable to you at this time. In other words, not too high—not too low. In this manner, you will have chosen a reasonable desire and your belief will accept it, making you worthy. Now, this desire is ready to be planted through your Imagination. The following methods will show you how.

_____THE METHODS

There are four main methods I use. I suggest you practice all of them and give each one a chance to work. Each will open the "secret door" (your Imagination) in a way you never thought possible.

NOTE: You must realize that the Higher Force is like someone who speaks another language. Both the Higher Force and person can understand the same picture but they can't necessarily understand the same words.

## METHOD #1: SEMI-SLEEP

I have found that this method is the easiest to use. However, it's important to realize the exact moment that you are in the state of "limbo" that semi-sleep can produce. It will last for just a few minutes, perhaps even seconds, and you must take advantage of the allotted time to plant, through your Imagination, the desires that you wish the Higher Force to carry out.

Semi-sleep is that brief period of "serenity" you experience just before actual sleep and at the moment of awakening. If possible, train yourself to "go to sleep—wake up—go to sleep—wake up," etc. In between is the time you use to communicate with the Higher Force through your Imagination and plant your desires! During these brief periods of semi-sleep you can almost reach out and "feel" your desires entering through your Imagination—to emerge later—not as dreams but as reality!

## _____CHOOSE YOUR SURROUNDINGS CAREFULLY.

When using the semi-sleep method, it's important to give yourself every chance to make it as effective as possible. You might find that a couch is better than a bed, simply because a couch is not a "designated" sleeping place and sleep is not usually as deep as it is while lying in bed. On the other hand, if you prefer to use the method in bed, then by all means do so. You may even find that leaving the TV or stereo on is conducive to experiencing those periods of "limbo." The rise and fall of voices and tones can act as "wake-uppers" as you continually drift in and out of sleep. The important thing is, to use these periods of semi-sleep to plant desires through your Imagination.

## METHOD #2: MUSIC

The magic power of music has never been given full credit, although it's been used since ancient civilization for a variety of purposes, including communication. Only recently have the beneficial effects of music found their way into our everyday lives. Dentists use music and the "sounds of nature" to soothe their patients; music is heard in the operating rooms of hospitals and every doctor's office employs soft background music. In addition, music is heard whenever a relaxing atmosphere is needed in business or pleasure environments.

Since music has therapeutic value, then it can certainly be conducive to act as a catalyst between the Spiritual and the Physical.

## _____CHOOSE THE MUSIC THAT BEST SUITS YOU

With this method, the music can be of any type, as long as it allows you to communicate with the Higher Force through your Imagination. If possible, use earphones. In this way, you cut out all outside distractions. You become an intimate threesome: You, the Music and your Imagination!

With the Music Method, it's not necessary to go in and out of sleep. The music will have such an effect that it will create its own "limbo" state of semi-consciousness and allow you to freely use your Imagination.

After a sufficient period of time you will feel wonderfully refreshed and have renewed energy. You will have planted your desires through your Imagination and you will KNOW you have reached the Higher Force within you and the things you desire will come to you because NOW they already exist! Remember—**Everything manmade was first a thought and then a thing.** At the moment you imagine it, the Higher Force creates it.

## METHOD #3: IMAGINATION WITH POSITIVE ACTION

This is a method you can use many times a day. When you develop your own techniques to bring it about, you will be able to accomplish your desires very easily. In Part II of this book you will find various visual aids to help you develop "positive action" habits. Simply stated, Imagination With Positive Action is the fastest way to turn your desires into reality.

_____FAST ACTION—FAST RESULTS

Let me illustrate the method of Imagination With Positive Action with two examples. The first is a common occurrence most of us experience quite often. If you are inside your house and you wish to go to your car which is parked in the driveway, you instantly communicate through your Imagination and plant the desire of going to the car. Why? Simply because you have no doubt.

_____YOU HAVE ABSOLUTE FAITH AND BELIEF

You KNOW what you want and you KNOW you can achieve it. This is the very foundation of going beyond your subconscious! You imagine, in a millionth of a second, that you ARE going to your car—and you GO! In fact, you can't move from the spot where you are right now unless you have a desire to do so. Elementary? Of course, but then, "great truths" are always very simple. The point is, by taking Positive Action you communicate with the Higher Force through your Imagination and follow through.

The second example of Imagination With Positive Action is a little more subtle and dramatic, as the following story illustrates:

_____*THE RAINMAKER*

Once there was a farmer. Year after year he enjoyed successful crops. Then came a drought and his crops started to wither and die. Each night he sat at his kitchen table, "imagining" it to rain; conjuring all sorts of thoughts; "seeing" it raining in his mind's eye; imagining the skies to become full with rain clouds.

One morning he ventured out, looking for the first raindrops. But there was no rain; in fact, it was hotter than ever. He looked at his fields but all he saw was dust in the wind. He turned back and went inside, cursing the Higher Force who, he thought, had let him down. For all intents and purposes, he lost all faith and hope in life itself.

Later that same day, his friend, also a farmer, visited him from a few miles away. He was overcome with joy because he, too, had imagined it raining and, sure enough, it did and his crops were saved. The farmer who had lost everything bitterly asked why it didn't rain on his crops, also. The other farmer politely asked if he had taken his umbrella with him when he stepped outside. His friend assured him he had. "Did you OPEN it?" asked the other. Sheepishly, the farmer who lost everything admitted he had not. When he didn't open his umbrella he was saying, in effect, that he never really **believed** that what he was doing was going to work, anyway. He didn't have true faith and belief that it would rain, as did his neighbor. He had "imagined" in vain. The moral of the story is: When you imagine it raining, open your umbrella when you step outside.

The same principle holds true with other things you

desire in life. If you imagine them and truly KNOW that they already exist, they WILL come to you. But if you don't have that inner faith and belief, then you have wasted your time. You have not used your Imagination to your benefit and felt the sensation of fulfillment, the true knowledge that you have allowed the powerful force within you to give you the things you want. It's the development of absolute faith and belief. With this you can do anything! It's one thing to TAKE your umbrella when you HOPE it will rain. It's another thing to OPEN your umbrella because you KNOW it will rain.

## METHOD #4: MEDITATION

Meditation is a natural process inherent in mankind. Without fully realizing it, we all meditate many times a day if only for a few fleeting moments. It's the time we take to pause and reflect; to think about everything from job security to whether or not we should invest in the stock market. We momentarily take our minds off current matters and ponder the unknown.

There are countless ways to meditate and we devise new methods constantly. Over the years, I've developed a simple method that works very well and I suggest that you try it.

## YOU AND THE POWER

The time you spend communicating through your Imagination with meditation is vitally important and you must do everything possible to make it the most effective that you can. These are private moments to be shared by you and the Higher Force. They belong to no one else. You must get rid of as many distractions as possible and properly prepare your mind and body for your "spiritual rendezvous."

## THE SETTING

I suggest that you set aside a specific room or area in which to meditate and use it daily to communicate with the Higher Force through your Imagination. Also, by choosing a certain location you will establish a habit and stick with the method.

It's helpful to create an atmosphere of tranquility. Although I do not believe that physical objects possess magical or mystical powers, the use of incense and candles can do much to impart a "relaxing aura" within your surroundings and help induce the feeling of contentment and serenity that is necessary. Sometimes, soft background music can do much to add to the tranquil scene. As pointed out in the Music Method, dentists use "nature sounds" to soothe their patients' fears. I strongly urge you to incorporate the same method. There are a number of cassettes available that range from the sound of ocean waves to the soft chirping of birds. By shopping around a bit, you'll be able to choose the sounds that best put you in the proper frame of mind.

## DEEP BREATHING

Once you have established your special area, it's time to prepare yourself physically for the actual meditation. We all know how important it is to breathe properly. Health experts tell us we should do deep breathing exercises daily to help keep in shape. I've discovered that deep breathing can actually change your state of mind in a matter of seconds, making meditation easier to accomplish. With a little practice, you can learn how to breathe properly, being careful not to hyperventilate and become dizzy or disoriented.

## HOW TO DO IT PROPERLY

Inhale slowly, from the pit of the stomach, and expand the lungs to their fullest. Now, hold the breath for a moment, then exhale gradually. Through practice, I've found that FIVE deep breaths are adequate for myself; however, this could vary with the individual. Take your time and establish the right number of breaths that seem comfortable to you. You can take these breaths while lying down, standing or seated in a chair. Your body will become completely relaxed. In as few as thirty seconds all the tensions of the day can disappear and you will then be ready to communicate your desires.

## MAKE IT A DAILY HABIT

IMPORTANT NOTE: With all methods, you should set aside the same time each day to practice them. By doing so, they will become more effective.

Once you set aside these private moments of communication, you will become more at peace with yourself and the Higher Force within you. It is during these private moments that you can employ one or more of the techniques discussed in Part Two of this book. When using the Meditation Method, I suggest you practice IMAGIVISION™. (Technique #6: Imagivision-the Mental Movie.)™

_____ _OTHER METHODS_

There are other methods you can incorporate in your daily practice. They can help you reach the force within you more easily in conjunction with the four main methods I've outlined.

You can open the "secret door" (your Imagination) while taking a leisurely bath or prolonged shower. As the warm water relaxes your body and eases the tensions you have built up, allow your mind to wander; let it drift beyond the subconscious. Pretend that what you desire is already yours—and it will be!

There are many other ways to open the "secret door". I'm quite sure you will discover even more exciting ways than I have. It could be while jogging or other exercise, or while taking a casual stroll in the early morning or late evening hours. As stated earlier, I can communicate with the Higher Force through my Imagination in almost any situation. You can, too!

_____SUMMATION

1. The "Pins and Needles" sensation is the one you experience when your Inner Self communicates with your Outer Self. It's not necessary to feel the pins and needles sensation to get the things you want. Some people experience it—some do not. When it happens, it will take place with no conscious effort on your part.

2. There are four main methods to consider when you wish to communicate with the Higher Force through your Imagination:

   A. Method #1: Semi-Sleep

   B. Method #2: Music

   C. Method #3: Imagination With Positive Action

   D. Method #4: Meditation

3. There are other methods. You can also develop your own to act as tools for the main four.

# THERE
# IS NO
# ADVERSITY

*"There Is No Adversity
If You Take
Positive Action."*

_____*THE MARK OF FAILURE*

When I tell people there is no such thing as "adversity," they look at me as though I have lost my mind. I assure you I haven't. Unfortunately, it's those people who constantly complain about their "bad luck" in life who fail. They believe that adversity haunts them and has singled them out to torment them and hold them back from achieving their desires. Don't get me wrong. At one time, I also believed this hogwash!

I used to sit back and envy those people who had made a success of themselves and came to the conclusion that it would never happen to me because I was marked with the "stigma of failure." I had accepted my lot in life and considered myself lucky to have a mediocre job that would put a little food on the table and pay the rent. How wrong I was! As stated earlier, once I discovered the secret, nothing could hold me back. That's why I refuse to recognize "adversity." You should, too, once you understand what it really is . . . or, more correctly, isn't.

## _MOOD SWINGS_

Don't confuse "adversity" with mood swings which are a natural part of the human make-up. We all have our "good days" and "bad days." It seems that no matter how hard we try, we experience periods of sadness, depression and misunderstanding. Now and then we all wake up on the wrong side of the bed. It's human nature. We're in a bad mood and nothing seems to go right. The important thing to remember is, YOU CANNOT CHANGE THE DAY BUT ONLY THE WAY YOU LOOK AT IT.

## _TAKE POSITIVE ACTION_

When you feel as though your life is falling to pieces, you must assess your situation and take positive action. If your ceiling falls in on your head, don't sit there and cry; get up and rebuild it. If you take positive action, then there is no adversity. This is how a negative is turned into a positive. (The new ceiling is now better than the old ceiling!)

## _USE YOUR MOOD SWINGS TO BEST ADVANTAGE_

I have discovered that when I'm in a good mood, or an "up cycle," it's the best time to communicate my desires through my Imagination and insert still more **positive** ideas. In this way I maintain a constant level of fulfillment and contentment and actually reduce the "depth" of the down cycles that are a part of normal living. Unfortunately, too many people, when in a down cycle, become humble. They get down on their hands and knees, meditate and imagine and, by a stroke of fate, get out of the mess they are in and heave a big sigh of relief. Then what do they do when things turn around? They stop meditating and imagining and become laid-back and self-satisfied. They tell themselves this good fortune will last forever. What happens? Before they know it, misfortune strikes and they are right back in a down cycle, on their hands and knees again.

What they should do is stay humble even in their "up-cycle" and constantly thank the Higher Force which gave them the things they have.

By constantly taking positive action, adversity ceases to exist. Look at adversity as nature's way of motivating you. Constantly remind yourself that when you're in a "good" mood, it is the best time to communicate your desires through your Imagination. On the other hand, when you're in a down cycle, try to weather the storm and wait it out. (You can't do your best thinking in a down cycle, anyway.) It won't last long and if you look at it from a "positive" attitude instead of a "negative" one, it will pass all the more quickly and will actually strengthen you. Remember that everything great in life is accomplished by overcoming "adversity:" The birth of a nation; the scaling of a mountain; the discovery of a medical breakthrough, etc. So, whenever you're faced with adversity, say to yourself, "There is no adversity if I take positive action."

## THE SIMPLE SOLUTION
## TO ALL YOUR PROBLEMS

There is no adversity! What happened was nature's way of moving you upward, bettering your position. At the time, you may not realize this but in the future it will become clear. This is the reason for taking positive action. With this knowledge, there is no reason to dwell in misery.

**Get on with your life!**

**Don't sit there and cry!**

**Start rebuilding!**

What just took place will help you. It's a blessing in disguise.

## *HOW TO TURN NEGATIVE SITUATIONS INTO POSITIVE OPPORTUNITIES*

**Negative Situation:** You just lost your job.

**Positive Opportunity:** Look forward to your next job. This might seem difficult to do but losing your job really presents you with an opportunity to better yourself. You probably weren't truly happy with your old job. Deep down, you decided you didn't want it because **YOU** control your future whether you admit it or not!

Your Imagination is the "Secret Door." Imagine yourself getting a bigger paycheck at your new job and being much happier. Nurture this desire with faith and belief and allow the Higher Force within you to give you this job which exists—right now!

**Negative Situation:** You have a handicap.

**Positive Opportunity:** Never look at a "handicap" as **being** one, but, rather, an opportunity to use your talents to their full advantage. We all are aware of how great people can become by ignoring their so-called handicaps and turning them into assets. Having a handicap presents us with even greater opportunities than those without them, simply

because we are more highly motivated.
Therefore, when communicating with the
Higher Force within you, imagine yourself "emerging" from your shell of self-
pity and utilizing the many talents you
have that were suppressed. With true
faith and belief, you can do anything.
Once you really understand life, you will
realize there is no such thing as a handicap, anyway.

| | |
|---|---|
| Negative Situation: | You are experiencing poverty. |
| Positive Opportunity: | Being put into poverty certainly makes us humble. However, many of us don't real-ize what we missed and go through life without experiencing the gratifying feel-ing of being "humble!" Even though you might be broke, poverty can give you spiritual depth and the opportunity to discover the Higher Force. This could cause you to have a spiritual awakening and find the true meaning of life, giving you a totally new perspective and out-look. It's true. Poverty is a valuable learn-ing experience, even though we don't wish to stay at that level. Be happy that you have known poverty because now you realize it's nature's way of motivating you. Now, take advantage of it. The Higher |

Force within you has a plan for your desires. Communicate what you desire through your Imagination.

**Negative Situation:** Your mate just divorced you.

**Positive Opportunity:** Divorce, or separation, can be one of the most devastating and heart-breaking situations we can encounter in life. Yet, this too can be turned into a Positive Opportunity, if only we allow the Higher Force within us to let it happen. We must first realize that we cannot "force" that other person to change their mind. If the divorce or separation is obviously going to be permanent, then there is no sense in dwelling in misery. Realize that you didn't marry the "right" person and there is someone else destined to be your mate—the **right** one. "Order" a new mate through your Imagination.

The right person will come into your life at the right time and the right place—automatically—and you will live happily ever after.

**Negative Situation:** You have just suffered the death of a loved one.

**Positive Opportunity:** Look upon that loved one as being freed from the Physical world. Their thoughts and deeds will live on in the Mental and the Spiritual, since that's really what they were from the beginning. Remember, we are Spiritual Beings pretending to be Physical Beings.

Our loved ones never really leave us; they are always present—our memories of them, their kindly acts, their encouraging words and love. Let the grief run its natural course while we cherish the legacy of their momentary stay on Earth. After all, we are just passing by on our journey through eternity.

NOTE: If anything, they should grieve for us because we must still continue OUR journey in the Physical world.

## LIFE IS FULL OF OPPORTUNITIES

If you change your way of thinking and look upon "adversity" as nature's way of motivating you to higher things, then adversity will, indeed, cease to exist for you. It might seem difficult at first, especially when life has just dealt you a "cruel" blow. But, look around you. When you look closely, you'll discover you are not alone by any means. All of us are confronted by obstacles every day and they range from small ones to gigantic "burdens" that seem insurmountable. The old saying, "When the going gets tough, the tough get going," is certainly appropriate in today's hectic society. Just make sure you "get going" in the right manner and use the powerful force within you wisely. If you do, then you can truly say: "THERE IS NO ADVERSITY!"

_____SUMMATION

1. We all have good days and bad days; up and down cycles. Look at them as opportunities to use your mood swings to best advantage. It's better to communicate with the Higher Force through your Imagination on your good days rather than bad days, because you will do your best thinking when you're in an "up" cycle.

2. There is no adversity if you take positive action.

3. Adversity is nature's way of motivating us.

4. Always look for ways to turn a **negative** into a **positive.**

# THE HIGHER FORCE

## vs.

# THE LOWER FORCE

"I Am *You*.
*You Are Me.*
*We Are* One."

_____*THE "I AM"*

Once you have acquired the various methods of going beyond your subconscious mind to communicate your desires through your Imagination, it's vitally important to know the difference between the Higher and Lower Forces that can prevail as you achieve your desires. It's unfortunate, but it is possible to achieve your desires from a Lower Force if you allow the Physical Self to be in control. Therefore, before you continue, read the following warning:

## WARNING

YOU HOLD IN YOUR HANDS THE MOST POWERFUL INFORMATION EVER POSSESSED BY MANKIND. AS YOU LEARN HOW TO USE THIS INFORMATION, BE CAREFUL NOT TO INFRINGE ON THE RIGHTS OF OTHER PEOPLE. WITHIN YOU IS A POWER THAT KNOWS WHAT YOU DESIRE. BY USING THIS POWER PROPERLY, YOU WILL BE FULFILLED AND EXPERIENCE TRUE PEACE OF MIND.

The main problem with allowing the Physical Self, or more aptly, the Lower Force, to give you the things you want is that it usually results in hurting someone else. On the other hand, by allowing the Higher Force to give you the things you desire, everyone benefits. You must imagine only what you desire, not the source or the means. The Lower Force works by being selfish and possessive. The Higher Force works in a way unknown to all of us. The Lower Force can be used to give you the things you want but they are temporary and eventually, in one way or another, will be taken from you.

To further illustrate the difference between allowing the Physical to be in control versus the Spiritual, I have compiled a brief list. On the left are the results of allowing the Physical to be in control. On the right is what happens when you allow the Spiritual to take control:

| PHYSICAL | SPIRITUAL |
| --- | --- |
| Evil | Good |
| Sad | Happy |
| Poverty | Wealth |
| Loser | Winner |
| Backward | Forward |
| I Benefit | Everyone Benefits |
| Darkness | Light |
| I Lead My Life | A Higher Force Leads Me |
| Help Me | Help Others |
| Anger | Peace |
| Hate | Love |
| Cheat | Honesty |
| Take | Give |

| | |
|---|---|
| Hopelessness | Hope |
| Depression | Joy |
| Impossible | Everything is Possible |
| Wrong | Right |
| I Am Me | I Am Everything |
| Illness | Health |
| I Am My Own Keeper | I Am My Brother's Keeper |
| Self | Us |

Therefore, the conclusion to be drawn is that there is a right way and a wrong way to obtain the things you desire. The main thing to remember when imagining is to never desire the possessions of others. This is greed and although it may benefit you temporarily, it will hurt others and eventually be taken from you. Any history book tells us that.

Let us briefly discuss the wrong way and right way of obtaining a few things in life most of us desire. Following are some situations you may have experienced, or will experience later in life:

SITUATION NO. 1: Looking for the "Perfect" Mate

WRONG WAY: You imagine or "picture" someone you know. You attempt to force something to happen by allowing your "I AM" to take control within your Physical Self. You consciously "look" for your "specific" mate—even, perhaps, desiring someone else's mate.

RIGHT WAY: Allow the Higher Force to give you who you want. When imagining your perfect mate, think of only the characteristics you desire such as personality, compatibility, etc. You can be assured that the Higher Force will give this mate to you and YOU have not caused it to happen!

SITUATION NO. 2:  Job Advancement

WRONG WAY:  You are employed by a company that promotes by merit. You wish to climb the corporate ladder and advance from your present position to a higher one. So, you "imagine" yourself getting someone else's job. Perhaps it's a coworker; your immediate supervisor, etc.

RIGHT WAY:  By getting that person's job you could be hurting others and eventually your actions will catch up with you in some way or another. Instead, imagine that your paycheck is bigger and you have received a promotion—one in which you see yourself as being happy.

SITUATION NO. 3:  Getting a New House

WRONG WAY:  You are driving along, looking for houses, when you spot a nice three bedroom home with a big front yard. The family is enjoying a summer day. The kids are playing on the swing; the father is trimming the neat-looking hedge while the mother is relaxing in a lawn chair, watching the children. What a happy scene! You say to yourself that you want this house and you secretly hope something happens to that family to enable you to get it. You "imagine" yourself being in possession of it. This is totally the wrong approach. By desiring someone else's possessions, great harm can come to them and you will pay for your actions in the future.

RIGHT WAY:    Forget about desiring a particular house that is occupied by owners who are obviously happy with it and don't want to lose it. Rather, "imagine" your dream house just the way you want it. Picture the number of bedrooms; how the kitchen will look; the front yard; the backyard; the living room; dining area; baths, etc. Choose what color you wish the house to be and the price range you are willing and able to pay. After you have done this, look at houses for

SALE—ones that the current owners no longer desire to possess. This way, when you find your dream house, everyone benefits; you haven't hurt anyone.

SITUATION NO. 4:  Possessing Nice Things

WRONG WAY:  It's fine to desire nice things in life: Shiny new cars, homes, yachts, vacations, just to name a few. But too many of us desire our neighbor's possessions. We become jealous and envious of our neighbor who is polishing his new Lincoln in his driveway; we look with dismay at our friend's new washer and dryer, etc. It is just as wrong to **desire** another's possessions as it is to **steal** them.

RIGHT WAY:  Imagine the things you want without regard to those owned by others. If you admire your next door neighbor's new car, then imagine that you will own a similar new car —not your neighbor's. Don't allow envy and jealousy to control you. Instead, allow the Higher Force within you to give you the reasonable things you want.

By now, I'm sure you understand the difference between allowing the Physical and Spiritual Selves to dominate and give importance to your life. When the Physical is in control, it wants to control others or what they have. It's important, therefore, not to base your desires on greed by wanting the possessions of others, but rather, to communicate to the Higher Force through your Imagination what you desire without infringing on the rights of others. The history of the world is rampant with people who had only selfish Physical motives. Without exception, their deeds caught up with them and they ended in failure. Heed the warning stated earlier in this chapter and make sure you use the methods and techniques in "Beyond The Subconscious" in the proper manner in which they are intended. I have never acquired anything through greed or through a desire to own someone else's possessions. I hope you do likewise. By using the information prudently and wisely, you will attain your wishes and desires by communicating through your Imagination. The Higher Force that dwells within you will cause these things to happen and make itself known to you.

I hope you have absorbed the information in these seven brief chapters and have realized what the "true secret" is. The Techniques and Tools which follow in Part Two will further strengthen your grasp and understanding. YOU ARE NOW ON THE THRESHOLD OF YOUR NEW BEGINNING.

_____SUMMATION

1. Both the Lower Force and the Higher Force can give you the things you want.

2. The Lower Force comes from the Physical Self and is based on greed.

3. By using the Spiritual Self, the things you receive will benefit everyone; whereas the things received from the Physical Self will hurt others.

4. Things received from the Physical Self will be eventually taken from you in some manner.

5. Use the methods and techniques carefully and in the proper manner and you will achieve true peace of mind.

# PART TWO

# BEYOND THE SUBCONSCIOUS

# TECHNIQUES
# &
# TOOLS

# LIST OF TECHNIQUES

## TECHNIQUE #1:
### You, Inc. Over 100 Desires™

## TECHNIQUE #2:
### Imagination Deposit Slips™

## TECHNIQUE #3:
### ImagiCards™

## TECHNIQUE #4:
### Ticket To Success™

## TECHNIQUE #5:
### Success Formula™

## TECHNIQUE #6:
### Imagivision—The Mental Movie™

## TECHNIQUE #7:
### Self-Evaluation Check List—
### The Mental Mirror™

The seven special Techniques and Tools that follow are designed to complement the four main methods outlined in Chapter Five. They can also be used by themselves. It is up to you to form a daily program of Imagination. With a little innovation on your part, you will be able to structure your program to suit your moods and allotted time periods.

Each Technique will work somewhat in the same manner. You might wish to use one of them for a period of time, such as a week, a month or longer, then switch to another Technique. Your own experimentation is the best guide.

_____*IMPORTANT ADVICE*

Before practicing these Techniques, it's vitally important to understand the following:

- You don't need to take anyone else's possessions.

- You don't need to hurt anyone in any way, shape or form.

- When the Higher Force works, it NEVER takes from anyone or hurts anyone. That's the beauty of using these Techniques—something higher gives us what we desire.

- You'll know you're not doing the right thing if other people get hurt. If you take other people's possessions, and they don't benefit as a result, you are allowing the Lower Force to grant your desire as opposed to the Higher Force.

- Heed the advice in Chapter Seven concerning the Lower Force versus the Higher Force and keep it in mind when practicing all Techniques. This is so vitally important that you will see the following WARNING preceding each Technique:

## WARNING

IF THIS TECHNIQUE IS NOT USED PROP-
ERLY; IF YOU ATTEMPT TO OVERPOWER
OTHER PEOPLE IN ORDER TO ATTAIN
YOUR DESIRE, YOU WILL HAVE TO REC-
TIFY THE WRONGS YOU HAVE DONE
MANY TIMES OVER. LET YOUR CON-
SCIENCE BE YOUR GUIDE.

TECHNIQUE #1

# YOU, INC. ™
# Over 100 Desires

*"Success Is Doing—*
*Not Wishing."*

## ——————————————THE WISHERS AND THE DOERS

Everybody has hundreds of desires. The problem is, we never bother to write them down. Therefore, this first technique is meant to separate the "wishers" from the "doers." To put it another way, "Success is **doing,** not **wishing."** You can wish from now till the end of time but mere wishing "upon a star" will get you nothing but an empty dream.

Look upon yourself as a "company" with yourself as president. Organize your life like a business. Can you imagine a business as being successful without organization? No desires, no files, no set times—"come and go" as you please? It's doubtful that you'll find such a business because, more than likely, it's OUT of business!

## ——————————————ORGANIZE A FILE SYSTEM

Since every successful business keeps accurate files, you should, too. Get a file box and some file folders (or make some from cardboard) and start getting specific about your life. Good health is an important desire, so you might start your first file on the subject of "Health."

Collect all the data you can on Health. Clip out news articles on diets; new advances in medicine, etc. Jot down notes on television news highlighting health; visit your local library and read the latest books on health. You'll be amazed at how much you'll learn! Before you know it, you will acquire a lot of information about your own body and be in a much better position to attain a more healthful attitude and to practice good health habits. You are **doing** —not **wishing!** You are becoming a winner instead of a loser.

Don't stop with one file. Remember, you are a SPE-CIAL corporation and you have many jobs ("desires") to do. Start a file on your financial condition; one for important dates; insurance, etc. In time, you will have made an impressive set of folders and you can look upon it as a tremendous accomplishment, one of which you can be proud for years to come. You will actually be turning your life around; organizing it until, one by one, you receive all your reasonable desires.

In addition to the major desires in your life, you should have other desires; minor ones that bring you happiness and peace of mind. (Remember, there is an awesome force within you that is waiting to give you all the reasonable things you want. Only YOU can release this power that lies locked within you!)

In order to bring about the many desires of your life, it's vitally important, again, to make a thorough list and make file folders for them. Just for the fun of it, I have listed over one hundred desires. You may have even more—or, perhaps, less. The important thing is, write them down on paper. This will crystallize your thoughts.

# EXAMPLE

## _____YOU, INC. OVER ONE HUNDRED DESIRES
### CHECK-OFF DESIRES AND LIST DATES AS YOU RECEIVE THEM.

1. Good Health
2. Visit Paris
3. Sky-Dive
4. Visit London
5. Go Back Packing
6. Go Camping
7. Plant A Garden
8. Visit Niagara Falls
9. Go Horseback Riding
10. Snow Skiing
11. Cross Country Skiing
12. Scuba Diving
13. Mountain Climbing
14. Visit Disneyland
15. Visit Disney World
16. Visit New York City
17. Paint The House
18. Take Karate Lessons
19. Take Dance Lessons
20. Take Bike Trip
21. Stop Smoking
22. Ride In Helicopter
23. Hot Air Balloon Ride
24. Visit San Paolo
25. Get Better Job
26. Find A Mate/Soulmate
27. Get New Car
28. Get Sailboat
29. Buy New VCR
30. Buy Tape Recorder
31. Lose Weight
32. Buy New Clothes
33. Make A Quilt
34. Gain Weight
35. Buy A House
36. Visit Hawaii
37. Visit Italy
38. See Martha's Vineyard
39. Write Short Stories
40. Go Canoeing
41. See Super Bowl Game
42. Be On TV
43. Invent Something
44. Go To Las Vegas
45. Visit Yellowstone
46. Visit China
47. Visit Tibet
48. Visit Japan
49. Visit Thailand
50. Take Ocean Cruise
51. Visit Europe
52. See Grand Canyon
53. Visit India
54. Visit Africa

# EXAMPLE

## _____YOU, INC. OVER ONE HUNDRED DESIRES

CHECK-OFF DESIRES AND LIST DATES AS YOU RECEIVE THEM.

| | |
|---|---|
| 55. Visit Vietnam | 82. Go To Mardi Gras |
| 56. Visit Australia | 83. Play Golf/Take Lessons |
| 57. Visit Sweden/Denmark | 84. Learn To Sew |
| 58. Visit My Birthplace | 85. Learn Ceramics |
| 59. Visit My Hometown | 86. Join Health Club |
| 60. Visit Russia | 87. Do Volunteer Work |
| 61. Visit Holland | 88. Further Education |
| 62. See Pyramids in Egypt | 89. Try Hang Gliding |
| 63. Visit Greece | 90. Go Spelunking |
| 64. Write A Book | 91. Visit Mammoth Cave |
| 65. Remodel A House | 92. Visit Washington D.C. |
| 66. Get A Motorcycle | 93. Be In A Movie |
| 67. Run In A Marathon | 94. Take A Train Trip |
| 68. Learn Magic Tricks | 95. Visit Mexico |
| 69. Play The Piano | 96. Visit South America |
| 70. Be A Gourmet Cook | 97. Get Married |
| 71. Get In Guinness Book | 98. Go On A Space Flight |
| 72. Have Children | 99. Learn Ice-Skating |
| 73. Learn Another Language | 100. Go Roller-Skating |
| 74. Win A Contest | 101. See A Broadway Play |
| 75. Visit Alaska | 102. Learn To Drive |
| 76. Prospect For Gold | 103. Meet A Celebrity |
| 77. Collect Antiques | 104. Live To Be Over 100 |
| 78. Start Coin Collection | 105. Start Bottle Collection |
| 79. Start Stamp Collection | 106. Speed Walking |
| 80. Go Fishing | 107. Scout Leader |
| 81. Learn Photography | 108. Tennis Lessons |

# _____YOU, INC. OVER ONE HUNDRED DESIRES

**CHECK-OFF DESIRES AND LIST DATES AS YOU RECEIVE THEM.**

1. _____
2. _____
3. _____
4. _____
5. _____
6. _____
7. _____
8. _____
9. _____
10. _____
11. _____
12. _____
13. _____
14. _____
15. _____
16. _____
17. _____
18. _____
19. _____
20. _____
21. _____
22. _____
23. _____
24. _____
25. _____
26. _____
27. _____
28. _____
29. _____
30. _____
31. _____
32. _____
33. _____
34. _____
35. _____
36. _____
37. _____
38. _____
39. _____
40. _____
41. _____
42. _____
43. _____
44. _____
45. _____
46. _____
47. _____
48. _____
49. _____
50. _____
51. _____
52. _____
53. _____
54. _____

## _____YOU, INC. OVER ONE HUNDRED DESIRES

CHECK-OFF DESIRES AND LIST DATES AS YOU RECEIVE THEM.

| | |
|---|---|
| 55. _____ | 82. _____ |
| 56. _____ | 83. _____ |
| 57. _____ | 84. _____ |
| 58. _____ | 85. _____ |
| 59. _____ | 86. _____ |
| 60. _____ | 87. _____ |
| 61. _____ | 88. _____ |
| 62. _____ | 89. _____ |
| 63. _____ | 90. _____ |
| 64. _____ | 91. _____ |
| 65. _____ | 92. _____ |
| 66. _____ | 93. _____ |
| 67. _____ | 94. _____ |
| 68. _____ | 95. _____ |
| 69. _____ | 96. _____ |
| 70. _____ | 97. _____ |
| 71. _____ | 98. _____ |
| 72. _____ | 99. _____ |
| 73. _____ | 100. _____ |
| 74. _____ | 101. _____ |
| 75. _____ | 102. _____ |
| 76. _____ | 103. _____ |
| 77. _____ | 104. _____ |
| 78. _____ | 105. _____ |
| 79. _____ | 106. _____ |
| 80. _____ | 107. _____ |
| 81. _____ | 108. _____ |

# _YOU, INC. OVER ONE HUNDRED DESIRES

### CHECK-OFF DESIRES AND LIST DATES AS YOU RECEIVE THEM.

| | |
|---|---|
| 1. _____ | 28. _____ |
| 2. _____ | 29. _____ |
| 3. _____ | 30. _____ |
| 4. _____ | 31. _____ |
| 5. _____ | 32. _____ |
| 6. _____ | 33. _____ |
| 7. _____ | 34. _____ |
| 8. _____ | 35. _____ |
| 9. _____ | 36. _____ |
| 10. _____ | 37. _____ |
| 11. _____ | 38. _____ |
| 12. _____ | 39. _____ |
| 13. _____ | 40. _____ |
| 14. _____ | 41. _____ |
| 15. _____ | 42. _____ |
| 16. _____ | 43. _____ |
| 17. _____ | 44. _____ |
| 18. _____ | 45. _____ |
| 19. _____ | 46. _____ |
| 20. _____ | 47. _____ |
| 21. _____ | 48. _____ |
| 22. _____ | 49. _____ |
| 23. _____ | 50. _____ |
| 24. _____ | 51. _____ |
| 25. _____ | 52. _____ |
| 26. _____ | 53. _____ |
| 27. _____ | 54. _____ |

## _____YOU, INC. OVER ONE HUNDRED DESIRES

**CHECK-OFF DESIRES AND LIST DATES AS YOU RECEIVE THEM.**

| | |
|---|---|
| 55. _____ | 82. _____ |
| 56. _____ | 83. _____ |
| 57. _____ | 84. _____ |
| 58. _____ | 85. _____ |
| 59. _____ | 86. _____ |
| 60. _____ | 87. _____ |
| 61. _____ | 88. _____ |
| 62. _____ | 89. _____ |
| 63. _____ | 90. _____ |
| 64. _____ | 91. _____ |
| 65. _____ | 92. _____ |
| 66. _____ | 93. _____ |
| 67. _____ | 94. _____ |
| 68. _____ | 95. _____ |
| 69. _____ | 96. _____ |
| 70. _____ | 97. _____ |
| 71. _____ | 98. _____ |
| 72. _____ | 99. _____ |
| 73. _____ | 100. _____ |
| 74. _____ | 101. _____ |
| 75. _____ | 102. _____ |
| 76. _____ | 103. _____ |
| 77. _____ | 104. _____ |
| 78. _____ | 105. _____ |
| 79. _____ | 106. _____ |
| 80. _____ | 107. _____ |
| 81. _____ | 108. _____ |

## _____YOU, INC. OVER ONE HUNDRED DESIRES
### CHECK-OFF DESIRES AND LIST DATES AS YOU RECEIVE THEM.

1. _____
2. _____
3. _____
4. _____
5. _____
6. _____
7. _____
8. _____
9. _____
10. _____
11. _____
12. _____
13. _____
14. _____
15. _____
16. _____
17. _____
18. _____
19. _____
20. _____
21. _____
22. _____
23. _____
24. _____
25. _____
26. _____
27. _____

28. _____
29. _____
30. _____
31. _____
32. _____
33. _____
34. _____
35. _____
36. _____
37. _____
38. _____
39. _____
40. _____
41. _____
42. _____
43. _____
44. _____
45. _____
46. _____
47. _____
48. _____
49. _____
50. _____
51. _____
52. _____
53. _____
54. _____

_____YOU, INC. OVER ONE HUNDRED DESIRES
CHECK-OFF DESIRES AND LIST DATES AS YOU RECEIVE THEM.

55. _____     82. _____
56. _____     83. _____
57. _____     84. _____
58. _____     85. _____
59. _____     86. _____
60. _____     87. _____
61. _____     88. _____
62. _____     89. _____
63. _____     90. _____
64. _____     91. _____
65. _____     92. _____
66. _____     93. _____
67. _____     94. _____
68. _____     95. _____
69. _____     96. _____
70. _____     97. _____
71. _____     98. _____
72. _____     99. _____
73. _____     100. _____
74. _____     101. _____
75. _____     102. _____
76. _____     103. _____
77. _____     104. _____
78. _____     105. _____
79. _____     106. _____
80. _____     107. _____
81. _____     108. _____

## _____YOU, INC. OVER ONE HUNDRED DESIRES
CHECK-OFF DESIRES AND LIST DATES AS YOU RECEIVE THEM.

1. _____
2. _____
3. _____
4. _____
5. _____
6. _____
7. _____
8. _____
9. _____
10. _____
11. _____
12. _____
13. _____
14. _____
15. _____
16. _____
17. _____
18. _____
19. _____
20. _____
21. _____
22. _____
23. _____
24. _____
25. _____
26. _____
27. _____

28. _____
29. _____
30. _____
31. _____
32. _____
33. _____
34. _____
35. _____
36. _____
37. _____
38. _____
39. _____
40. _____
41. _____
42. _____
43. _____
44. _____
45. _____
46. _____
47. _____
48. _____
49. _____
50. _____
51. _____
52. _____
53. _____
54. _____

## _____ YOU, INC. OVER ONE HUNDRED DESIRES
CHECK-OFF DESIRES AND LIST DATES AS YOU RECEIVE THEM.

55. _____     82. _____
56. _____     83. _____
57. _____     84. _____
58. _____     85. _____
59. _____     86. _____
60. _____     87. _____
61. _____     88. _____
62. _____     89. _____
63. _____     90. _____
64. _____     91. _____
65. _____     92. _____
66. _____     93. _____
67. _____     94. _____
68. _____     95. _____
69. _____     96. _____
70. _____     97. _____
71. _____     98. _____
72. _____     99. _____
73. _____     100. _____
74. _____     101. _____
75. _____     102. _____
76. _____     103. _____
77. _____     104. _____
78. _____     105. _____
79. _____     106. _____
80. _____     107. _____
81. _____     108. _____

©1988, THE IMAGINATION STORE, 2424 BEEKMAN ST., CINCINNATI, OH 45214

# ———YOU, INC. OVER ONE HUNDRED DESIRES

**CHECK-OFF DESIRES AND LIST DATES AS YOU RECEIVE THEM.**

1. _____
2. _____
3. _____
4. _____
5. _____
6. _____
7. _____
8. _____
9. _____
10. _____
11. _____
12. _____
13. _____
14. _____
15. _____
16. _____
17. _____
18. _____
19. _____
20. _____
21. _____
22. _____
23. _____
24. _____
25. _____
26. _____
27. _____
28. _____
29. _____
30. _____
31. _____
32. _____
33. _____
34. _____
35. _____
36. _____
37. _____
38. _____
39. _____
40. _____
41. _____
42. _____
43. _____
44. _____
45. _____
46. _____
47. _____
48. _____
49. _____
50. _____
51. _____
52. _____
53. _____
54. _____

_____YOU, INC. OVER ONE HUNDRED DESIRES

CHECK-OFF DESIRES AND LIST DATES AS YOU RECEIVE THEM.

55. _____  82. _____
56. _____  83. _____
57. _____  84. _____
58. _____  85. _____
59. _____  86. _____
60. _____  87. _____
61. _____  88. _____
62. _____  89. _____
63. _____  90. _____
64. _____  91. _____
65. _____  92. _____
66. _____  93. _____
67. _____  94. _____
68. _____  95. _____
69. _____  96. _____
70. _____  97. _____
71. _____  98. _____
72. _____  99. _____
73. _____  100. _____
74. _____  101. _____
75. _____  102. _____
76. _____  103. _____
77. _____  104. _____
78. _____  105. _____
79. _____  106. _____
80. _____  107. _____
81. _____  108. _____

## EXAMPLE

Let us say that your desire is to "visit Paris." The first thing you must do is start a file folder and collect all the information you need to know about Paris. How much will the total trip cost? What airline is offering the best travel plan? Get maps and books about the city. Start learning to speak the language. By doing these things you are crystallizing your thoughts and being specific about what you want. When the day finally arrives that you **do** visit Paris, you will be completely prepared for the trip. Your vacation will prove to be much more enjoyable than you ever expected.

Making file folders containing your desires is the first step toward getting them. After all, success is doing, not wishing. You can wish all you want but if you don't take steps to get what you want, then you'll probably never get it. It bears repeating over and over: The Higher Force within you is waiting NOW to give you anything you want. If you don't want anything then you won't get anything. WANT NOT—HAVE NOT!

## TECHNIQUE #1

1. Run yourself like a business.
2. Organize a file system for all of your desires.
3. List your desires to crystallize your thoughts.
4. Remember: If you don't ask for anything, you won't get anything. Want Not—Have Not.

**WARNING**

IF THIS TECHNIQUE IS NOT USED PROPERLY; IF YOU ATTEMPT TO OVERPOWER OTHER PEOPLE IN ORDER TO ATTAIN YOUR DESIRE, YOU WILL HAVE TO RECTIFY THE WRONGS YOU HAVE DONE MANY TIMES OVER. LET YOUR CONSCIENCE BE YOUR GUIDE.

# IMAGINATION DEPOSIT SLIPS™

*"What You Sow,*
*So Shall You Reap."*

## CRYSTALLIZING YOUR THOUGHTS

This Technique might look very simple, but as you fill in your desires, by writing them down on the Imagination Deposit slips, you are crystallizing your thoughts in the Physical. This is the beginning of all things. Your desires have been deposited through your Imagination and if you continuously nurture them with faith and belief and know that they already exist, you will have them in the Physical.

When you fill in the Imagination Deposit slips, examples of which follow, you are depositing your desires through your Imagination. You are letting your desires grow, somewhat like a bank account, until one magic day, your desires become reality. By using the Imagination Deposit slips, you will be able to enjoy in the Physical what you imagine in the Spiritual.

## MAKE A DATE WITH DESTINY

You'll notice there are two dates indicated on the stub of each Imagination Deposit slip. One indicates the date on which you made the deposit and the other indicates the date on which the item you deposited through your Imagination is returned to you in the Physical. These dates are important so don't just merely pick a date at random and fill in the slip without thought. You must be specific when you fill out the slip. First of all, before you fill in the date of deposit, make sure the item you deposit through your Imagination is within reason for you at the time. Once you have determined this, go ahead and fill in the slip, including the date of deposit. Be sure to list every detail you can think of concerning the item you wish to receive. This can be either a Physical item, such as a car; a Spiritual desire, such as a mate, or any other reasonable desire. The more specific you get, the better.

_____*THREE STEPS TO DESTINY*

You will also notice that the Imagination Deposit slip lists three important steps to take:

Step 1.  See yourself in possession of what you deposited.

Step 2.  Don't give up. Your deposit will come back to you in the Physical.

Step 3.  Enjoy in the Physical what you imagined.

The item you deposit could be returned to you in the Physical in a very short time. Then again, it might take quite awhile. That's why you should set a reasonable amount of time to attain your desire. Just keep seeing yourself in possession of what you deposited and, by all means, DON'T GIVE UP!

# EXAMPLES

Date 4-1-19??

Item Deposited New black Lincoln Town Car

Item returned to you in the physical
Lincoln Continental

Date 1-10-19??

**IMAGINATION DEPOSIT SLIP** Date 4-1-19??

Item to be deposited New black Lincoln Town Car with all accessories — sunroof — CB — stereo — power doors — power windows — whitewall tires.

STEP #1   See yourself in possession of what you deposited.

STEP #2   Don't give up. Your deposit will come back to you in the physical.

STEP #3   Enjoy in the physical what you imagined.

© 1988, THE IMAGINATION STORE, 2424 BEEKMAN ST., CINCINNATI, OH 45214

---

Date 6-9-19??

Item Deposited New house

Item returned to you in the physical
3-bedroom house — O.K.

Date 1-1-19??

**IMAGINATION DEPOSIT SLIP** Date 4-1-19??

Item to be deposited 4-bedroom house — w/3 baths — swimming pool — sauna — hot tub — 2 car attached garage — large lawn — shade trees — close to schools.

STEP #1   See yourself in possession of what you deposited.

STEP #2   Don't give up. Your deposit will come back to you in the physical.

STEP #3   Enjoy in the physical what you imagined.

© 1988, THE IMAGINATION STORE, 2424 BEEKMAN ST., CINCINNATI, OH 45214

---

Date 10-1-19??

Item Deposited Pay Raise

Item returned to you in the physical
45% a week — O.K.

Date 11-1-19??

**IMAGINATION DEPOSIT SLIP** Date 10-1-19??

Item to be deposited A raise in pay. 50% a week.

STEP #1   See yourself in possession of what you deposited.

STEP #2   Don't give up. Your deposit will come back to you in the physical.

STEP #3   Enjoy in the physical what you imagined.

© 1988, THE IMAGINATION STORE, 2424 BEEKMAN ST., CINCINNATI, OH 45214

## EXAMPLES

Date 2-4-19??
Item Deposited To make
the bowling team at work

**IMAGINATION DEPOSIT SLIP** Date 2-4-19??
Item to be deposited J want to make the bowling team
at work.

Item returned to
you in the physical
180 avg.
J made it
Date 5-6-19??

STEP #1   See yourself in possession of what you deposited.

STEP #2   Don't give up. Your deposit will come back to you in the physical.

STEP #3   Enjoy in the physical what you imagined.
© 1988, THE IMAGINATION STORE, 2424 BEEKMAN ST., CINCINNATI, OH 4521⁴

Date 4-20-19??
Item Deposited Sailboat

**IMAGINATION DEPOSIT SLIP** Date _____
Item to be deposited A Sailboat with all the trimmings:
A cabin with galley that seats four comfortably. Three sails.
A dinghy. A transmitter for sea-to-shore communication.
Apx. length: 32 ft. Cost: $???

Item returned to
you in the physical
Sailboat

Date 8-19-19??

STEP #1   See yourself in possession of what you deposited.

STEP #2   Don't give up. Your deposit will come back to you in the physical.

STEP #3   Enjoy in the physical what you imagined.
© 1988, THE IMAGINATION STORE, 2424 BEEKMAN ST., CINCINNATI, OH 4521⁴

Date 12-4-19??
Item Deposited Health
Club

**IMAGINATION DEPOSIT SLIP** Date _____
Item to be deposited Join Health Club. Workout with
another group on a weekly basis. Specialize in aerobics. Meet
new friends. Get back in condition. Lose ## lbs. Tone
up stomach muscles and get rid of "love handles"
around waist.

Item returned to
you in the physical
Membership

Date 1-6-19??

STEP #1   See yourself in possession of what you deposited.

STEP #2   Don't give up. Your deposit will come back to you in the physical.

STEP #3   Enjoy in the physical what you imagined.
© 1988, THE IMAGINATION STORE, 2424 BEEKMAN ST., CINCINNATI, OH 4521⁴

Date _____    **IMAGINATION DEPOSIT SLIP** Date _____
Item Deposited _____   Item to be deposited _____
_____   _____
_____   _____
_____   _____
_____   _____

                        | STEP #1   See yourself in possession of what you
Item returned to        |           deposited.
you in the physical     | STEP #2   Don't give up. Your deposit will come back
_____   |           to you in the physical.
_____   | STEP #3   Enjoy in the physical what you imagined.
Date _____    |   © 1988, THE IMAGINATION STORE, 2424 BEEKMAN ST., CINCINNATI, OH 45214

Date _____    **IMAGINATION DEPOSIT SLIP** Date _____
Item Deposited _____   Item to be deposited _____
_____   _____
_____   _____
_____   _____
_____   _____

                        | STEP #1   See yourself in possession of what you
Item returned to        |           deposited.
you in the physical     | STEP #2   Don't give up. Your deposit will come back
_____   |           to you in the physical.
_____   | STEP #3   Enjoy in the physical what you imagined.
Date _____    |   © 1988, THE IMAGINATION STORE, 2424 BEEKMAN ST., CINCINNATI, OH 45214

Date _____    **IMAGINATION DEPOSIT SLIP** Date _____
Item Deposited _____   Item to be deposited _____
_____   _____
_____   _____
_____   _____
_____   _____

                        | STEP #1   See yourself in possession of what you
Item returned to        |           deposited.
you in the physical     | STEP #2   Don't give up. Your deposit will come back
_____   |           to you in the physical.
_____   | STEP #3   Enjoy in the physical what you imagined.
Date _____    |   © 1988, THE IMAGINATION STORE, 2424 BEEKMAN ST., CINCINNATI, OH 45214

Date _____

Item Deposited _____

_____

_____

_____

_____

Item returned to
you in the physical

_____

_____

Date _____

---

**IMAGINATION DEPOSIT SLIP** Date _____

Item to be deposited _____

_____

_____

_____

STEP #1    See yourself in possession of what you deposited.

STEP #2    Don't give up. Your deposit will come back to you in the physical.

STEP #3    Enjoy in the physical what you imagined.

© 1988, THE IMAGINATION STORE, 2424 BEEKMAN ST., CINCINNATI, OH 45214

---

Date _____

Item Deposited _____

_____

_____

_____

_____

Item returned to
you in the physical

_____

_____

Date _____

---

**IMAGINATION DEPOSIT SLIP** Date _____

Item to be deposited _____

_____

_____

_____

STEP #1    See yourself in possession of what you deposited.

STEP #2    Don't give up. Your deposit will come back to you in the physical.

STEP #3    Enjoy in the physical what you imagined.

© 1988, THE IMAGINATION STORE, 2424 BEEKMAN ST., CINCINNATI, OH 45214

---

Date _____

Item Deposited _____

_____

_____

_____

_____

Item returned to
you in the physical

_____

_____

Date _____

---

**IMAGINATION DEPOSIT SLIP** Date _____

Item to be deposited _____

_____

_____

_____

STEP #1    See yourself in possession of what you deposited.

STEP #2    Don't give up. Your deposit will come back to you in the physical.

STEP #3    Enjoy in the physical what you imagined.

© 1988, THE IMAGINATION STORE, 2424 BEEKMAN ST., CINCINNATI, OH 45214

Date _____
Item Deposited _____
_____
_____
_____
_____

Item returned to
you in the physical
_____
_____
Date _____

**IMAGINATION DEPOSIT SLIP** Date _____
Item to be deposited _____
_____
_____
_____
_____

STEP #1   See yourself in possession of what you deposited.

STEP #2   Don't give up. Your deposit will come back to you in the physical.

STEP #3   Enjoy in the physical what you imagined.

© 1988, THE IMAGINATION STORE, 2424 BEEKMAN ST., CINCINNATI, OH 45214

---

Date _____
Item Deposited _____
_____
_____
_____
_____

Item returned to
you in the physical
_____
_____
Date _____

**IMAGINATION DEPOSIT SLIP** Date _____
Item to be deposited _____
_____
_____
_____
_____

STEP #1   See yourself in possession of what you deposited.

STEP #2   Don't give up. Your deposit will come back to you in the physical.

STEP #3   Enjoy in the physical what you imagined.

© 1988, THE IMAGINATION STORE, 2424 BEEKMAN ST., CINCINNATI, OH 45214

---

Date _____
Item Deposited _____
_____
_____
_____
_____

Item returned to
you in the physical
_____
_____
Date _____

**IMAGINATION DEPOSIT SLIP** Date _____
Item to be deposited _____
_____
_____
_____
_____

STEP #1   See yourself in possession of what you deposited.

STEP #2   Don't give up. Your deposit will come back to you in the physical.

STEP #3   Enjoy in the physical what you imagined.

© 1988, THE IMAGINATION STORE, 2424 BEEKMAN ST., CINCINNATI, OH 45214

Date _____

Item Deposited _____

_____

_____

_____

Item returned to
you in the physical

_____

_____

Date _____

**IMAGINATION DEPOSIT SLIP** Date _____

Item to be deposited _____

_____

_____

_____

STEP #1   See yourself in possession of what you
deposited.

STEP #2   Don't give up. Your deposit will come back
to you in the physical.

STEP #3   Enjoy in the physical what you imagined.

© 1988, THE IMAGINATION STORE, 2424 BEEKMAN ST., CINCINNATI, OH 45214

---

Date _____

Item Deposited _____

_____

_____

_____

Item returned to
you in the physical

_____

_____

Date _____

**IMAGINATION DEPOSIT SLIP** Date _____

Item to be deposited _____

_____

_____

_____

STEP #1   See yourself in possession of what you
deposited.

STEP #2   Don't give up. Your deposit will come back
to you in the physical.

STEP #3   Enjoy in the physical what you imagined.

© 1988, THE IMAGINATION STORE, 2424 BEEKMAN ST., CINCINNATI, OH 45214

---

Date _____

Item Deposited _____

_____

_____

_____

Item returned to
you in the physical

_____

_____

Date _____

**IMAGINATION DEPOSIT SLIP** Date _____

Item to be deposited _____

_____

_____

_____

STEP #1   See yourself in possession of what you
deposited.

STEP #2   Don't give up. Your deposit will come back
to you in the physical.

STEP #3   Enjoy in the physical what you imagined.

© 1988, THE IMAGINATION STORE, 2424 BEEKMAN ST., CINCINNATI, OH 45214

_____SUMMATION

## TECHNIQUE #2

1. Write down your desires to crystallize your thoughts. This is the beginning of all things.

2. Nurture them with faith and belief and **know** that they already exist.

3. Make out the date of deposit and the date your desire is returned in the Physical.

4. Take three steps to destiny:

   Step 1. See yourself in possession of what you deposited.

   Step 2. Don't give up. Your deposit will come back to you in the Physical.

   Step 3. Enjoy in the Physical what you imagined.

**WARNING**

IF THIS TECHNIQUE IS NOT USED PROPERLY; IF YOU ATTEMPT TO OVERPOWER OTHER PEOPLE IN ORDER TO ATTAIN YOUR DESIRE, YOU WILL HAVE TO RECTIFY THE WRONGS YOU HAVE DONE MANY TIMES OVER. LET YOUR CONSCIENCE BE YOUR GUIDE.

# IMAGICARDS™

*"Want Not—Have Not."*

## ALLOWING SUFFICIENT TIME

A goal can be described as the shortest distance between two points—from A to B. So it is with our desires. The purpose of life is to go from A to B, C to D and so on. Without desires, there is no reason to exist. Without desires we cannot move from A to B; we can't even move an inch. With IMAGICARDS, desires become more specific and are put in the proper perspective.

The problem many of us encounter with our desires is that we don't allow sufficient time for them to transpire, or, we don't make them reasonable enough. Sometimes we give up just a few hours before they are due to take place, thus eliminating them. Therefore, it's important to follow basic steps in determining our desires. Over the years, I've developed five basic steps which serve as my criteria for making a desire:

## HOW TO MAKE A DESIRE

Step 1.   What is your desire? (Make it reasonable.)

Step 2.   Set a reasonable amount of time to acquire this desire.

Step 3.　What are you going to give in return for this desire being granted?

Step 4.　What makes you worthy of receiving this desire?

Step 5.　Write down your desire to crystallize your thoughts.

_____GETTING YOUR DESIRE

Before you study the IMAGICARDS which follow later, let me explain the difference between making reasonable desires and unreasonable desires.

It's an easy task for most of us to walk a plank that's a foot off the ground. We know we can do it because we have absolutely no doubt in our minds. However, if we move the plank fifty feet off the ground we become filled with fear, doubt and frustration, unless, of course, we are acrobats and have allowed ourselves enough time to work up to that height. Therefore, keep your desires out of the clouds and close to the ground; close to reality where you can almost reach out and touch them, because you know they are there and you can get them.

A MENTAL PICTURE IS WORTH MORE
_____THAN A THOUSAND WORDS

This saying has true meaning when it comes to imagining your desires. Through your Imagination you must "see, hear, touch, smell and feel" your desires as if they are already in your possession. Let me illustrate this with the black Lincoln Town Car we deposited earlier via the Imagination Deposit slip. This time we will use an IMAGICARD which lists not only the item with its Desires but also the Motives for achieving the item.

Your desire is a Lincoln Town Car. Well, you will get a Lincoln Town Car but what kind? It might be a new Lincoln Town Car or an old Lincoln Town Car. It might not even run! Therefore, it's obvious that you must be more specific in your desire. The powerful force within you will certainly give you what you want, so you better be careful in your selection. Therefore, list exactly what you want your Lincoln Town Car to be.

How about a brand new black four-door Lincoln Town Car with wire wheels? Fine. List these things on your IMAGICARD. Add A/C, AM-FM Stereo, a CB, plus an in-car phone and you're in business. Don't forget the price and the fact that you "see" yourself driving up to a friend's house in your Lincoln. These are all the things you desire your item to be.

_____*MOTIVES*

You must also have definite motives for attaining your Lincoln Town Car. These might include better gas mileage; a comfortable ride; "dependability; provides the look and smell of success and is good for your image."

_____*ACT LIKE YOU OWN IT*

Just as you should make file folders for your desires, you

must also do things in connection with achieving those desires. In the case of the Lincoln Town Car, you must assume you own it—RIGHT NOW! Buy things for it, like a can of car wax or air freshener. Get some maps for the trips you're going to take. Get a Lincoln Town Car key chain; go to a car dealer and actually sit behind the wheel of one! Constantly think of owning and driving your new Lincoln. See it in your Imagination like a mini-motion picture. See yourself driving up to your friends and having them compliment you on your new car.

## TIMING

There is one more important element in getting your desire which shouldn't be overlooked. It's TIMING. If you work seriously with your Imagination, the force within you will see to it that you think properly; know what to say and when to say it and to be in the right place at the right time. It's true. When we are programmed for success, we cannot fail as long as we have faith and belief. The Higher Force will make sure that you will be in the right place at the right time, saying the right thing. You will have no control over this action; you will have fulfilled your desire whether you like it or not.

## LUCK

Many people think luck plays a big part in their desires.

Who knows what "luck" really is? True, a very small percentage of people win at the lottery but the vast majority fail. Even a smaller percentage win at the races and at poker games. But these are not true desires but merely **wishful thinking** and indulging in them can be catastrophic. It's literally throwing your fate to the winds and you should NEVER make your desires dependent on luck. There are millions of people right at this moment who ask "Lady Luck" to guide them to success. They will probably continue to dwell in their own misery and poverty until the day they die. How fortunate it would be if they learned how to communicate through their Imagination and allow the Higher Force to give them the things they want!

Now, take a few moments to examine the IMAG-ICARDS filled out for your guidance. With them you will be able to fill out your own IMAGICARDS and get the reasonable things you've been wanting.

*EXAMPLES OF IMAGICARDS*
*WITH DESIRES AND MOTIVES*

## IMAGICARD

**ITEM:**   Car

**D** 1.   Black Lincoln Town Car

**E** 2.   Four Door

**S** 3.   Wire Wheels

**I** 4.   New: Cost Apx.???

**R** 5.   A/C — FM-AM Stereo — CB

**E** 6.   In car phone

**S** 7.   Sunroof

**ITEM:**   Car

**M** 1.   Seats six comfortably

**O** 2.   Comfortable ride

**T** 3.   I look successful

**I** 4.   Car has that "smell of success"

**V** 5.   Dependable

**E** 6.   Good for my image

**S** 7.   Safety

## IMAGICARD

**ITEM:** Vacation

D 1. Sarasota, Florida

E 2. Rent two bedroom furnished condominium

S 3. Less than ??? per week

I 4. Visit Disney World and Epcot Center

R 5. Visit Busch Gardens

E 6. Collect seashells on the beach

S 7. Upon return, people say you have a good tan

**ITEM:** Vacation

M 1. Reward yourself for good work

O 2. See new places

T 3. Do new things

I 4. Share new experiences with family

V 5. Meet new people

E 6. Need change in climate

S 7. Get good tan and look healthier

## IMAGICARD

**ITEM:**   Stop Smoking

**D**  1.  Longer, healthier life

**E**  2.  Taste the flavor of food again

**S**  3.  Better self image

**I**  4.  Have fresher breath

**R**  5.  Have whiter teeth

**E**  6.  Run mile with no great pain

**S**  7.  Feel lungs improve

**ITEM:**   Stop Smoking

**M**  1.  Fear of lung cancer

**O**  2.  Better Smile

**T**  3.  No nicotine on teeth or fingers

**I**  4.  No bad smell in car or home

**V**  5.  No dirty, smelly ashtrays

**E**  6.  Save money

**S**  7.  No second hand smoke in children's lungs

_____*IMAGICARDS*

# IMAGICARD

**ITEM:**   **Health**

D   1.   Doing Aerobics

E   2.   Eating well balanced meals

S   3.   Getting proper sleep

I   4.   Taking long walk through woods

R   5.   Weigh less than ???

E   6.   Visualize yourself in perfect health

S   7.   People say how healthy you look

**ITEM:**   **Health**

M   1.   Live longer

O   2.   Live better quality of life

T   3.   Feel physically better

I   4.   Look better

V   5.   Lower insurance rate

E   6.   Fewer medical bills

S   7.   Feel younger

## IMAGICARD

**ITEM:**   Mate _____

D   1.   Attractive _____

E   2.   Likes camping _____

S   3.   People saying what a good couple we are ___

I   4.   Enjoys hiking, outdoors and travel _____

R   5.   Likes aerobics _____

E   6.   Positive thinker _____

S   7.   We romantically love each other _____

**ITEM:**   Mate _____

M   1.   A companion _____

O   2.   Avoid loneliness _____

T   3.   A friend and playmate _____

I   4.   Have children _____

V   5.   Someone to share my desires _____

E   6.   Share responsibility _____

S   7.   Need to care for another person _____

## IMAGICARD

**ITEM:**   Lose Weight
_____

- **D**   1.   Weigh under ???
- **E**   2.   Clothes will fit better
- **S**   3.   Feel better
- **I**   4.   People comment on how thin I look
- **R**   5.   Look better in mirror to myself
- **E**   6.   Breath easier
- **S**   7.   Tie shoes more easily (bend more easily)

**ITEM:**   Lose Weight
_____

- **M**   1.   Live longer
- **O**   2.   Do aerobics better
- **T**   3.   No more stomach pains
- **I**   4.   Having more energy
- **V**   5.   Hike better
- **E**   6.   More spiritually motivated
- **S**   7.   Have a better appearance

## IMAGICARD

**ITEM:** Job _____

   **D**  1.  Good pay (relative to job)

   **E**  2.  Tell someone you like your job

   **S**  3.  Get along with others at work

   **I**  4.  See yourself getting promotion

   **R**  5.  Good working conditions

   **E**  6.  Good location (within ?? miles from home)

   **S**  7.  See yourself getting annual bonus

**ITEM:** Job _____

   **M**  1.  Live more comfortably

   **O**  2.  Have fun working

   **T**  3.  Work with people you like to be around

   **I**  4.  Grow in experience and knowledge

   **V**  5.  Send children to college

   **E**  6.  Secure retirement plan

   **S**  7.  Good emotional attitude and emotional health

# IMAGICARD

**ITEM:**   House
_____

| | | |
|---|---|---|
| **D** | 1. | New four bedroom, yellow house/white trim |
| **E** | 2. | Cost less than ???? |
| **S** | 3. | Two fireplaces and large family room |
| **I** | 4. | On a no outlet street |
| **R** | 5. | Over ?? acres |
| **E** | 6. | Large garden area |
| **S** | 7. | Have family reunion at new house |

**ITEM:**   House
_____

| | | |
|---|---|---|
| **M** | 1. | Live more comfortably |
| **O** | 2. | Within budget??? |
| **T** | 3. | Tax write off |
| **I** | 4. | Privacy |
| **V** | 5. | Room for children and pets |
| **E** | 6. | Grow garden |
| **S** | 7. | Room for house guests |

## IMAGICARD

**ITEM:**   Take Train Trip _____

D   1.   Travel by train to: _____

E   2.   Trip to cost: $ _____

S   3.   Sleep in Pullman car _____

I   4.   Meet new friends during trip _____

R   5.   Enjoy fine meals in dining car _____

E   6.   Go through quaint towns and cities _____

S   7.   Ride in engineer's cab _____


**ITEM:**   Take Train Trip _____

M   1.   Learn more about America _____

O   2.   Chance to relax—slowdown the pace _____

T   3.   Learn something about passenger trains _____

I   4.   Have a chance to reflect upon life's meaning

V   5.   Use trip to communicate with Higher Force

E   6.   Have the time to write letters to friends _____

S   7.   Catch up on reading books and periodicals

_____IMAGICARDS

## IMAGICARD

**ITEM:**    **Future Person**

**D**   1.   Healthy

**E**   2.   Successful

**S**   3.   Self-Confident

**I**   4.   Interact more with family

**R**   5.   Read more

**E**   6.   Eat better

**S**   7.   New hairdo or cut

**ITEM:**    **Future Person**

**M**   1.   To have a better life

**O**   2.   To have a better life

**T**   3.   To have a better life

**I**   4.   To have a better life

**V**   5.   To have a better life

**E**   6.   To have a better life

**S**   7.   To have a better life

_____*IMAGICARDS*

## IMAGICARD

**ITEM:** _____

**D**  1. _____

**E**  2. _____

**S**  3. _____

**I**  4. _____

**R**  5. _____

**E**  6. _____

**S**  7. _____


**ITEM:** _____

**M**  1. _____

**O**  2. _____

**T**  3. _____

**I**  4. _____

**V**  5. _____

**E**  6. _____

**S**  7. _____

_____*IMAGICARDS*

## IMAGICARD

**ITEM:** _____

**D** 1. _____

**E** 2. _____

**S** 3. _____

**I** 4. _____

**R** 5. _____

**E** 6. _____

**S** 7. _____

**ITEM:** _____

**M** 1. _____

**O** 2. _____

**T** 3. _____

**I** 4. _____

**V** 5. _____

**E** 6. _____

**S** 7. _____

_____*IMAGICARDS*

## IMAGICARD

**ITEM:** _____

D 1. _____

E 2. _____

S 3. _____

I 4. _____

R 5. _____

E 6. _____

S 7. _____

**ITEM:** _____

M 1. _____

O 2. _____

T 3. _____

I 4. _____

V 5. _____

E 6. _____

S 7. _____

_____IMAGICARDS

## IMAGICARD

**ITEM:** _____

**D  1.** _____

**E  2.** _____

**S  3.** _____

**I  4.** _____

**R  5.** _____

**E  6.** _____

**S  7.** _____


**ITEM:** _____

**M  1.** _____

**O  2.** _____

**T  3.** _____

**I  4.** _____

**V  5.** _____

**E  6.** _____

**S  7.** _____

_____IMAGICARDS

## IMAGICARD

**ITEM:** _____

D   1. _____

E   2. _____

S   3. _____

I   4. _____

R   5. _____

E   6. _____

S   7. _____

**ITEM:** _____

M   1. _____

O   2. _____

T   3. _____

I   4. _____

V   5. _____

E   6. _____

S   7. _____

_____SUMMATION

## TECHNIQUE #3

1. Without desires there is no reason to exist.
2. There are 5 steps in making a desire:

   Step 1. What is your desire? (Make it reasonable.)

   Step 2. Set a reasonable amount of time to acquire this desire.

   Step 3. What are you going to give in return for this desire being granted?

   Step 4. What makes you worthy of receiving this desire?

   Step 5. Write down your desire to crystallize your thoughts.

3. A mental picture is worth more than a thousand words. With IMAGICARDS you become specific with your Desires and Motives for achieving them.

**WARNING**

IF THIS TECHNIQUE IS NOT USED PROP-
ERLY; IF YOU ATTEMPT TO OVERPOWER
OTHER PEOPLE IN ORDER TO ATTAIN
YOUR DESIRE, YOU WILL HAVE TO REC-
TIFY THE WRONGS YOU HAVE DONE
MANY TIMES OVER. LET YOUR CON-
SCIENCE BE YOUR GUIDE.

# TICKET
# TO SUCCESS™

*"Success Is No Accident—*
*It Happens On Purpose."*

## WRITE YOUR OWN TICKET

With this technique you can write your own Ticket To Success. Again, as a reminder, it's not necessary for you to use all the various techniques and methods described in this book. They are merely guides to use at your discretion. As mentioned before, each method and technique has been carefully planned and designed for maximum efficiency. They act as physical manifestations for communicating with the Higher Force through your Imagination more effectively. This particular technique, Ticket To Success, can be used in conjunction with one of your main methods or by itself. This is true of the other methods and techniques. It is up to you to use your own judgment as to which methods and techniques are best suited for your particular needs at any specific time.

_____*TICKET TO SUCCESS*

## EXAMPLE

**INSTRUCTIONS:**
- Fill in the spaces below.
- Enter this desire through your Imagination. Know that this will be given to you and see yourself in possession of what you desired. Repeat this process over and over until your desire is given to you.
- **Important:** Your desire must be reasonable, or when it is entered through your Imagination, you will see failure instead of success and you will not receive it.

**TODAY'S DATE:** _July 10_ 19 _??_.

**DESIRE TO HAPPEN BEFORE:** _Dec. 25_ 19 _??_.

**WHAT IS DESIRED:**

_A new house — 4 bedrooms — blue trim — 2 car_

_garage — cost: ??? 3 acres — wooded area nice_

_neighborhood._

_____

_____

_____

I hereby agree to continue imagining my desire as being in my possession until it is given to me. I also understand that the average person fails because they give up too soon.

**SIGNED:** _Marilyn Doe_ **DATE:** _March 4_ 19 _??_.

———————————————————————*TICKET TO SUCCESS*

## EXAMPLE

**INSTRUCTIONS:**
- Fill in the spaces below.
- Enter this desire through your Imagination. Know that this will be given to you and see yourself in possession of what you desired. Repeat this process over and over until your desire is given to you.
- **Important:** Your desire must be reasonable, or when it is entered through your Imagination, you will see failure instead of success and you will not receive it.

TODAY'S DATE: _Apr. 8_ 19 _??_.

DESIRE TO HAPPEN BEFORE: _July 14_ 19 _??_.

WHAT IS DESIRED:

_Learn magic tricks. Examples: How to saw a_
_lady-in-half trick; pull rabbit out of hat; make_
_bird disappear in cage; create illusions;_
_suspend someone in air. Become well-known_
_as magician and be hired by groups for_
_entertainment._

I hereby agree to continue imagining my desire as being in my possession until it is given to me. I also understand that the average person fails because they give up too soon.

SIGNED: _Harold Jones_ DATE: _April 8_ 19 _??_.

_____*TICKET TO SUCCESS*

## INSTRUCTIONS:
- Fill in the spaces below.
- Enter this desire through your Imagination. Know that this will be given to you and see yourself in possession of what you desired. Repeat this process over and over until your desire is given to you.
- **Important:** Your desire must be reasonable, or when it is entered through your Imagination, you will see failure instead of success and you will not receive it.

TODAY'S DATE: _____ 19 ___.

DESIRE TO HAPPEN BEFORE: _____19 ___.

WHAT IS DESIRED:

_____

_____

_____

_____

_____

_____

I hereby agree to continue imagining my desire as being in my possession until it is given to me. I also understand that the average person fails because they give up too soon.

SIGNED: _____ DATE: _____ 19 ___.

_____*TICKET TO SUCCESS*

## INSTRUCTIONS:
- Fill in the spaces below.
- Enter this desire through your Imagination. Know that this will be given to you and see yourself in possession of what you desired. Repeat this process over and over until your desire is given to you.
- **Important:** Your desire must be reasonable, or when it is entered through your Imagination, you will see failure instead of success and you will not receive it.

TODAY'S DATE: _____ 19 ___.

DESIRE TO HAPPEN BEFORE: _____19 ___.

WHAT IS DESIRED:

_____

_____

_____

_____

_____

     I hereby agree to continue imagining my desire as being in my possession until it is given to me. I also understand that the average person fails because they give up too soon.

SIGNED: _____ DATE: _____ 19 ___.

_____ _TICKET TO SUCCESS_

## INSTRUCTIONS:
- Fill in the spaces below.
- Enter this desire through your Imagination. Know that this will be given to you and see yourself in possession of what you desired. Repeat this process over and over until your desire is given to you.
- **Important:** Your desire must be reasonable, or when it is entered through your Imagination, you will see failure instead of success and you will not receive it.

TODAY'S DATE: _____ 19 ___.

DESIRE TO HAPPEN BEFORE: _____19 ___.

WHAT IS DESIRED:

_____

_____

_____

_____

_____

_____

I hereby agree to continue imagining my desire as being in my possession until it is given to me. I also understand that the average person fails because they give up too soon.

SIGNED: _____ DATE: _____ 19 ___.

———————————————————————*TICKET TO SUCCESS*

## INSTRUCTIONS:

- Fill in the spaces below.
- Enter this desire through your Imagination. Know that this will be given to you and see yourself in possession of what you desired. Repeat this process over and over until your desire is given to you.
- **Important:** Your desire must be reasonable, or when it is entered through your Imagination, you will see failure instead of success and you will not receive it.

TODAY'S DATE: _____ 19 __ .

DESIRE TO HAPPEN BEFORE: _____ 19 __ .

WHAT IS DESIRED:

_____

_____

_____

_____

_____

_____

_____

    I hereby agree to continue imagining my desire as being in my possession until it is given to me. I also understand that the average person fails because they give up too soon.

SIGNED: _____ DATE: _____ 19 __ .

_____*TICKET TO SUCCESS*

## INSTRUCTIONS:

- Fill in the spaces below.
- Enter this desire through your Imagination. Know that this will be given to you and see yourself in possession of what you desired. Repeat this process over and over until your desire is given to you.
- **Important:** Your desire must be reasonable, or when it is entered through your Imagination, you will see failure instead of success and you will not receive it.

TODAY'S DATE: _____ 19 __.

DESIRE TO HAPPEN BEFORE: _____19 __.

WHAT IS DESIRED:

_____

_____

_____

_____

_____

_____

I hereby agree to continue imagining my desire as being in my possession until it is given to me. I also understand that the average person fails because they give up too soon.

SIGNED: _____ DATE: _____ 19 __.

_____*SUMMATION*

## TECHNIQUE #4

1. Before writing your own Ticket To Success, remember to make it reasonable. Otherwise, once it's entered through your Imagination, you will see failure instead of success. You will not receive your desire.

## WARNING

IF THIS TECHNIQUE IS NOT USED PROP-
ERLY; IF YOU ATTEMPT TO OVERPOWER
OTHER PEOPLE IN ORDER TO ATTAIN
YOUR DESIRE, YOU WILL HAVE TO REC-
TIFY THE WRONGS YOU HAVE DONE
MANY TIMES OVER. LET YOUR CON-
SCIENCE BE YOUR GUIDE.

# SUCCESS FORMULA™

*"Forward Motion*
*Produces*
*Controlled Results."*

## FOLLOWING THE LAWS OF NATURE

There are hundreds and hundreds of so-called "Formulas For Success" in this world of ours. Aristotle, Homer, Plato and Socrates probably spent most of their senior years devising success formulas for their students to follow. Such wise patriarchs as Benjamin Franklin, Thomas Jefferson and others carried on the tradition in early America. Today, learned writers constantly devise "magic steps" to success that promise riches and happiness beyond our wildest dreams.

This is all well and good. The problem is, these "formulas for success" merely rehash age-old concepts of "self-improvement, motivation, desire," etc. Using only two parts, the Physical and the Mental, they don't go beyond the subconscious. They do not open the "Secret Door" and use the power within us to grant the things wanted. These success formulas contain an aura of mystery and magic about them as if they were handed down from the ancients and concocted from rare elements. The truth is, there is no magic or mystery about success. If you control what goes into yourself, you can control the future—or—"We are today who we thought we were yesterday." Success simply boils down to the Law of Nature that says

"Any seed or thought planted in fertile soil or in a receptive mind and nurtured with true faith and belief, will mature and bear fruit." It is with this concept that I have devised a simple, straightforward formula which anyone can follow. Study the following samples, then make out one of your own.

_____SUCCESS FORMULA

## EXAMPLE

I know I am today who I thought I was yesterday. This is true because I control what goes into myself: My food, my thoughts and my beliefs. Therefore, by using my Imagination I know that I can have any reasonable thing I want. I also know that there is no magic or mystery in what I am doing. I am using the Law of Nature which states that any seed or thought planted in fertile soil or in a receptive mind and nurtured with true faith and belief, will mature and bear fruit.

**THEREFORE, I AM IMAGINING THIS DESIRE SO THAT IT CAN BE TURNED INTO A REALITY.**

Before: <u>Feb. 8</u> 19 ?? I KNOW I WILL HAVE IN MY POSSESSION:

<u>Over $75,000 in real estate</u>

This will be brought to me because it's the Law of Nature. I am so confident this will happen that I can see, hear, touch, smell and feel my desire. I realize that after I imagine my desire for a period of time, I will be given a plan from the Higher Force, so that what I desire can be brought to me. I also realize that by using all three parts of myself—Physical, Mental and Spiritual, and by repeating these statements daily with feeling and belief, my desire has already been given to me in the future.

Signed: <u>John Doe</u> Date: <u>Jan. 1</u>  19 ??

_____*SUCCESS FORMULA*

## EXAMPLE

I know I am today who I thought I was yesterday. This is true because I control what goes into myself: My food, my thoughts and my beliefs. Therefore, by using my Imagination I know that I can have any reasonable thing I want. I also know that there is no magic or mystery in what I am doing. I am using the Law of Nature which states that any seed or thought planted in fertile soil or in a receptive mind and nurtured with true faith and belief, will mature and bear fruit.

**THEREFORE, I AM IMAGINING THIS DESIRE SO THAT IT CAN BE TURNED INTO A REALITY.**

Before: <u>Feb. 8</u> 19 <u>??</u> I **KNOW I WILL HAVE IN MY POSSESSION:**

<u>A coin collection worth over $25,000.</u>

    This will be brought to me because it's the Law of Nature. I am so confident this will happen that I can see, hear, touch, smell and feel my desire. I realize that after I imagine my desire for a period of time, I will be given a plan from the Higher Force, so that what I desire can be brought to me. I also realize that by using all three parts of myself—Physical, Mental and Spiritual, and by repeating these statements daily with feeling and belief, my desire has already been given to me in the future.

Signed: <u>John Doe</u> Date: <u>Jan. 1</u>   19 <u>??</u>

_____*SUCCESS FORMULA*

I know I am today who I thought I was yesterday. This is true because I control what goes into myself: My food, my thoughts and my beliefs. Therefore, by using my Imagination I know that I can have any reasonable thing I want. I also know that there is no magic or mystery in what I am doing. I am using the Law of Nature which states that any seed or thought planted in fertile soil or in a receptive mind and nurtured with true faith and belief, will mature and bear fruit.

**THEREFORE, I AM IMAGINING THIS DESIRE SO THAT IT CAN BE TURNED INTO A REALITY.**

Before: _____ 19 __ I KNOW I WILL HAVE IN MY POSSESSION:

_____

_____

This will be brought to me because it's the Law of Nature. I am so confident this will happen that I can see, hear, touch, smell and feel my desire. I realize that after I imagine my desire for a period of time, I will be given a plan from the Higher Force, so that what I desire can be brought to me. I also realize that by using all three parts of myself—Physical, Mental and Spiritual, and by repeating these statements daily with feeling and belief, my desire has already been given to me in the future.

Signed: _____ Date: _____ 19 ____

212 BEYOND THE SUBCONSCIOUS

_____*SUCCESS FORMULA*

I know I am today who I thought I was yesterday. This is true because I control what goes into myself: My food, my thoughts and my beliefs. Therefore, by using my Imagination I know that I can have any reasonable thing I want. I also know that there is no magic or mystery in what I am doing. I am using the Law of Nature which states that any seed or thought planted in fertile soil or in a receptive mind and nurtured with true faith and belief, will mature and bear fruit.

**THEREFORE, I AM IMAGINING THIS DESIRE SO THAT IT CAN BE TURNED INTO A REALITY.**

Before: _____ 19 __ I KNOW I WILL HAVE IN MY POSSESSION:

_____

_____

This will be brought to me because it's the Law of Nature. I am so confident this will happen that I can see, hear, touch, smell and feel my desire. I realize that after I imagine my desire for a period of time, I will be given a plan from the Higher Force, so that what I desire can be brought to me. I also realize that by using all three parts of myself—Physical, Mental and Spiritual, and by repeating these statements daily with feeling and belief, my desire has already been given to me in the future.

Signed: _____ Date: _____ 19 ____

© 1988, THE IMAGINATION STORE, 2424 BEEKMAN ST., CINCINNATI, OH 45214

_____*SUCCESS FORMULA*

I know I am today who I thought I was yesterday. This is true because I control what goes into myself: My food, my thoughts and my beliefs. Therefore, by using my Imagination I know that I can have any reasonable thing I want. I also know that there is no magic or mystery in what I am doing. I am using the Law of Nature which states that any seed or thought planted in fertile soil or in a receptive mind and nurtured with true faith and belief, will mature and bear fruit.

**THEREFORE, I AM IMAGINING THIS DESIRE SO THAT IT CAN BE TURNED INTO A REALITY.**

Before: _____ 19 __ I KNOW I WILL HAVE IN MY POSSESSION:

_____

_____

This will be brought to me because it's the Law of Nature. I am so confident this will happen that I can see, hear, touch, smell and feel my desire. I realize that after I imagine my desire for a period of time, I will be given a plan from the Higher Force, so that what I desire can be brought to me. I also realize that by using all three parts of myself—Physical, Mental and Spiritual, and by repeating these statements daily with feeling and belief, my desire has already been given to me in the future.

Signed: _____ Date: _____ 19 ____

_____*SUCCESS FORMULA*

I know I am today who I thought I was yesterday. This is true because I control what goes into myself: My food, my thoughts and my beliefs. Therefore, by using my Imagination I **know** that I can have any reasonable thing I want. I also know that there is no magic or mystery in what I am doing. I am using the Law of Nature which states that any seed or thought planted in fertile soil or in a receptive mind and nurtured with true faith and belief, will mature and bear fruit.

**THEREFORE, I AM IMAGINING THIS DESIRE SO THAT IT CAN BE TURNED INTO A REALITY.**

Before: _____ 19 ___ **I KNOW I WILL HAVE IN MY POSSESSION:**

_____

_____

This will be brought to me because it's the Law of Nature. I am so confident this will happen that I can see, hear, touch, smell and feel my desire. I realize that after I imagine my desire for a period of time, I will be given a plan from the Higher Force, so that what I desire can be brought to me. I also realize that by using all three parts of myself—Physical, Mental and Spiritual, and by repeating these statements daily with feeling and belief, my desire has already been given to me in the future.

Signed: _____ Date: _____ 19 ____

_____*SUCCESS FORMULA*

I know I am today who I thought I was yesterday. This is true because I control what goes into myself: My food, my thoughts and my beliefs. Therefore, by using my Imagination I know that I can have any reasonable thing I want. I also know that there is no magic or mystery in what I am doing. I am using the Law of Nature which states that any seed or thought planted in fertile soil or in a receptive mind and nurtured with true faith and belief, will mature and bear fruit.

**THEREFORE, I AM IMAGINING THIS DESIRE SO THAT IT CAN BE TURNED INTO A REALITY.**

Before: _____ 19 __ I KNOW I WILL HAVE IN MY POSSESSION:

_____

_____

This will be brought to me because it's the Law of Nature. I am so confident this will happen that I can see, hear, touch, smell and feel my desire. I realize that after I imagine my desire for a period of time, I will be given a plan from the Higher Force, so that what I desire can be brought to me. I also realize that by using all three parts of myself—Physical, Mental and Spiritual, and by repeating these statements daily with feeling and belief, my desire has already been given to me in the future.

Signed: _____ Date: _____ 19 ____

© 1988, THE IMAGINATION STORE, 2424 BEEKMAN ST., CINCINNATI, OH 45214

# HOW TO MAKE THE LAWS OF NATURE WORK FOR YOU

## PART ONE

# "Planting The Seed"

*"You Can't Harvest The Crop*
*Until You Plant*
*The Seed."*

Everything on Earth is governed by the Laws of Nature. One such law states that all things begin small—then grow larger. For example, we cannot harvest a crop before we plant the seed. By the same token, we must first imagine our desires before we can have them.

Most of us are not as successful as we wish, simply because we don't follow the Laws of Nature. We expect life to give us something before we have even asked for it. To understand this clearly, compare the two squares on the opposite page. One is a seed; the other represents our desires. If we plant the seed in fertile soil, water it and look after it carefully, it will become a mature plant. Nature grows the plant; all we can do is plant the seed and care for the seedling.

The same principle holds true with our desires. If we have no desires, then we cannot expect the Laws of Nature to work for us. After all, the mind works just like the soil of the Earth. Any thought planted in a receptive mind, and nurtured by faith, will automatically gain momentum and manifest itself in the physical. It will happen. It's the Law of Nature.

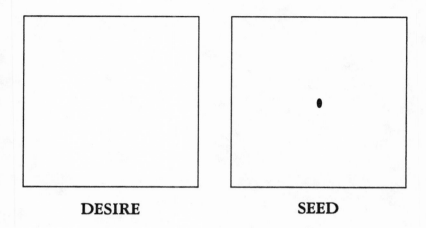

**DESIRE**              **SEED**

## HOW TO MAKE THE LAWS OF NATURE
## WORK FOR YOU

A. Prepare your mind. Have faith in what you are doing.

B. Make a reasonable desire. It's important that you write your desire on paper. This is the mental seed.

C. Nurture your desire with faith, knowing that what you have planted will "grow" and what you desired will happen because it's the Law of Nature.

D. Realize that your desire is growing and is already being manifested in the physical, little by little.

E. Thank the Higher Force for giving this to you and let nature take its course.

# HOW TO MAKE THE LAWS OF NATURE WORK FOR YOU

## PART TWO

# "In The Beginning"

IN THE BEGINNING there was but a single living cell. This cell divided and became two. The two cells became four and the cell continued to double upon itself until the Earth was filled with a multitude of living things.

The original cell still lives to this day and continues to double upon itself and will not die until the universe ceases to exist. All living things are a part of this cell and this cell is part of all living things. One is all; all is one. Its age is measured in billions of man-made years, yet it's but a fraction of a second if Eternity can be measured by time.

## THE DOUBLING EFFECT

This Law of Nature states that every living thing grows by "doubling upon itself." A human embryo, through the process of doubling its cells, actually "grows" millions and millions of new cells during the first few weeks of pregnancy. The huge coral reefs protecting the coastal lines of the seven continents are continuously being replenished by living cells. It's almost totally beyond belief how a tiny seed can sprout and keep doubling in size until it reaches maturity. And so it is with our desires in life. By planting the mental seed and nurturing it with faith and belief, it doubles upon itself until it emerges into reality. The "Doubling Effect" in nature can be mathematically illustrated by the following story which it would pay every young entrepreneur to read:

## THE FARMER AND THE YOUNG MAN

Once there was a farmer who owned a small herd of cows. Nearby lived a young man who thought he was very smart and wanted to make some money during the summer. He asked the farmer if he could milk his cows every day for a month. The farmer decided to test the lad, to see if he was really as smart as he claimed to be. He offered him the choice of two payment plans. Payment plan number one was a penny for the first day to be followed by two cents the second day, four cents the third day, eight cents the fourth day and so on. Each day, for thirty-one days, the farmer told him he would double the pennies. As the lad scratched his head, the farmer explained the second plan.

Rather than bothering with all those pennies, he would pay him five hundred dollars cash. The young man's eyes lit up and he immediately chose the five hundred dollars. At the end of the month, he proudly took home his money and showed it to his father. He then explained the first plan that the farmer had offered. His father, being wise, sat down to show his son how foolish he had been. Patiently, he wrote down the figures, day by day, doubling the total each time, for thirty-one days. The young entrepreneur, in disbelief, saw that he would have earned over ten million dollars!

Of course, if the lad had been smart enough to accept the "doubling plan," the farmer, no doubt, would have patted him on the back and congratulated him on being a brilliant young man...then offered him the five hundred dollars in cash. In any event, the story illustrates the process of "doubling" and this principle holds true with our desires. Once you plant the seed; once you put that first penny away, don't stop. Keep them growing and watch them double until you have a bumper crop, in the field or in the bank.

## THE DOUBLING EFFECT
### In Mathematics And Life

| | | | |
|---|---|---|---|
| 1. | $ .01 | 17. | 655.36 |
| 2. | .02 | 18. | 1,310.72 |
| 3. | .04 | 19. | 2,621.44 |
| 4. | .08 | 20. | 5,242.88 |
| 5. | .16 | 21. | 10,485.76 |
| 6. | .32 | 22. | 20,971.52 |
| 7. | .64 | 23. | 41,943.04 |
| 8. | 1.28 | 24. | 83,886.08 |
| 9. | 2.56 | 25. | 167,772.16 |
| 10. | 5.12 | 26. | 335,544.32 |
| 11. | 10.24 | 27. | 671,088.64 |
| 12. | 20.48 | 28. | 1,342,177.28 |
| 13. | 40.96 | 29. | 2,684,354.56 |
| 14. | 81.92 | 30. | 5,368,709.12 |
| 15. | 163.84 | 31. | $10,737,418.24 |
| 16. | $327.68 | | |

_____*WHERE DO YOU STAND?*

The Doubling Effect, portrayed above as money, can be interpreted in a variety of ways. For example, it can serve as a scale of values, measuring your status in life. Some of us settle for Step 10 and are content with "$5.12" worth of satisfaction. Others, being more ambitious, don't stop and continue to double their efforts until they reach a higher plateau. Of course, there is no ending. This is why we should always strive to do more good things in life and never settle for second best.

## TECHNIQUE #5

1. I am today who I thought I was yesterday.
2. I control what goes into myself: My food, my thoughts and my beliefs.
3. By using my Imagination, I can control my future.
4. I **know** that I can have any **reasonable** thing I want.
5. There is no magic or mystery in what I am doing.
6. I am using the Law of Nature which states that any seed or thought planted in fertile soil or in a receptive mind and nurtured with true faith and belief, will mature and bear fruit.

## WARNING

IF THIS TECHNIQUE IS NOT USED PROP-
ERLY; IF YOU ATTEMPT TO OVERPOWER
OTHER PEOPLE IN ORDER TO ATTAIN
YOUR DESIRE, YOU WILL HAVE TO REC-
TIFY THE WRONGS YOU HAVE DONE
MANY TIMES OVER. LET YOUR CON-
SCIENCE BE YOUR GUIDE.

# TECHNIQUE #6

# IMAGIVISION
# The Mental Movie™

*"The Force Within Me*
*Tells Me What To Do—*
*Because I Tell It What I Want."*

_____*YOU ARE THE STAR*

To me, this is one of the "fun" techniques that really produces fantastic results. It works best when using Method #1: Semi-Sleep or Method #2: Music. However, it could work for you with any method with which you feel the most comfortable.

Since most of us enjoy a good movie, either at a theatre or on television, this technique is perfectly suited to our purpose. Make sure you are in a completely relaxed mood. That's why I suggest you use the Semi-Sleep Method to bring it about. The examples which follow explain the technique in detail. It's up to you to write your own Imagivision Movie, then "act it out" through your Imagination. As stated in the examples, the Imagivision Movie begins at the end of the story. It only shows what you have accomplished—not how you did it.

When I use this technique, I spend quite a bit of time planning each ending scene in order to make it as exciting as I can. After all, most movies end in an exciting climax and Imagivision is no exception.

As with all techniques, please make sure your desire is reasonable for you at the time and give it a proper amount of time to happen. The ultimate "director-producer" within you will see to it that you will have a blockbuster of a movie and it will have a happy ending. In your case, it will be a new beginning.

_____*IMAGIVISION—THE MENTAL MOVIE*

## EXAMPLE

DATE <u>5-1-19??</u>

DESIRE: <u>(Be specific)</u> <u>Weight to be less than ???</u>

DATE: <u>before 8-2-19??</u>

The movie begins at the end of the story. It only shows what you have accomplished—not how you did it.

Scene 1: <u>It was almost too good to be true. I looked at the scale, it read ?? pounds. I felt light as a feather. My clothes felt so good, no more tight feeling. I bent over to tie my shoes and my stomach didn't hurt, from being pinched. That gave me a pins and needles feeling all over.</u>

Scene 2: <u>I walked into work and everyone started complimenting me, telling me how healthy and trim I look. I feel so much lighter, it's like I have springs on my feet. I notice I can do my job better now. I love being the right weight.</u>

Scene 3: <u>At the clothing store I noticed I had a much better selection available to me. Trying on new clothes and looking into the mirror, I really like who I see.</u>

Scene 4: <u>This is the first time I've been hiking since I lost all that weight. I can really feel the difference. I am climbing a steep hill now and hardly feel it. I feel good, I knew I could do it. Now that I eat right I will never have a weight problem again.</u>

_____IMAGIVISION—THE MENTAL MOVIE

## EXAMPLE

DATE <u>2-6-19??</u>

**DESIRE:** (Be specific) <u>To meet my perfect mate; one who is</u> <u>attractive; likes camping, hiking, outdoors and travel.</u> <u>Enjoys aerobics. Is a positive thinker who romantically</u> <u>loves me.</u>

**DATE:** <u>(To take place before: 19??)</u>

The movie begins at the end of the story. It only shows what you have accomplished—not how you did it.

**Scene 1:** <u>I never thought it was possible, but here I am with my</u> <u>special mate, the person I've wanted all my life. It's amazing how</u> <u>compatible we are. My mate likes most of the things I enjoy.</u>
**Scene 2:** <u>I can see a big difference in myself since I met my mate.</u> <u>I wake up happy in the morning, knowing I am going to spend the</u> <u>day with the one I love — sharing, giving, confiding — LOVING!</u>
**Scene 3:** <u>What a wonderful weekend we're planning! First, we're</u> <u>going to take a quiet walk in the woods, enjoying the solitude; taking</u> <u>in the fresh air. We'll eat a nice lunch around noon then head home.</u>
**Scene 4:** <u>My happiness knows no bounds! The very sight of my</u> <u>loved one sends chills up and down my spine. I want the whole</u> <u>world to know what a wonderful feeling it is to be with a person</u> <u>you cherish and in turn, that person cherishing you. If I live to</u> <u>be a hundred and ten, I will never be happier than I am right</u> <u>at this moment!</u>

_____*IMAGIVISION—THE MENTAL MOVIE*

## EXAMPLE

DATE _____

**DESIRE:** (Be Specific) _Stop smoking._ _____

_____

_____

**DATE:** _before ?-?-19??_

**The movie begins at the end of the story. It only shows what you have accomplished—not how you did it.**

**Scene 1:** _It's difficult to believe, but it's true! I know I will never smoke another cigarette again. It's been three months since I smoked my last cigarette and I feel great._

**Scene 2:** _For the first time since I can remember, my clothes don't smell like cigarette smoke. In fact, the whole house smells fresh._

**Scene 3:** _I went jogging this past weekend and I felt like I could run in a marathon. My breathing is so much easier since I quit smoking and I wake up each morning full of energy and pep._

**Scene 4:** _I had a checkup at the doctor's office and my chest x-rays were perfect. The doctor told me I probably added ten to twenty years to my life by stopping smoking._

## _____IMAGIVISION—THE MENTAL MOVIE

DATE _____

**DESIRE:** _____
_____
_____

**DATE:** _____

The movie begins at the end of the story. It only shows what you have accomplished—not how you did it.

Scene 1: _____
_____
_____

Scene 2: _____
_____
_____

Scene 3: _____
_____
_____

Scene 4: _____
_____
_____

_____*IMAGIVISION—THE MENTAL MOVIE*

DATE _____

DESIRE: _____
_____
_____

DATE: _____

The movie begins at the end of the story. It only shows what you have accomplished—not how you did it.

Scene 1: _____
_____
_____
_____

Scene 2: _____
_____
_____
_____

Scene 3: _____
_____
_____
_____

Scene 4: _____
_____
_____
_____

## *IMAGIVISION—THE MENTAL MOVIE*

DATE _____

DESIRE: _____
_____
_____

DATE: _____

The movie begins at the end of the story. It only shows what you have accomplished—not how you did it.

Scene 1: _____
_____
_____

Scene 2: _____
_____
_____

Scene 3: _____
_____
_____

Scene 4: _____
_____
_____

_____IMAGIVISION—THE MENTAL MOVIE

DATE _____
DESIRE: _____
_____
_____

DATE: _____

The movie begins at the end of the story. It only shows what you have accomplished—not how you did it.

Scene 1: _____
_____
_____
_____

Scene 2: _____
_____
_____
_____

Scene 3: _____
_____
_____
_____

Scene 4: _____
_____
_____
_____

## —————————IMAGIVISION—THE MENTAL MOVIE

DATE _____

**DESIRE:** _____
_____
_____

**DATE:** _____

The movie begins at the end of the story. It only shows what you have accomplished—not how you did it.

Scene 1: _____
_____
_____
_____

Scene 2: _____
_____
_____
_____

Scene 3: _____
_____
_____
_____

Scene 4: _____
_____
_____
_____

_____IMAGIVISION—THE MENTAL MOVIE

DATE _____

DESIRE: _____
_____
_____

DATE: _____

The movie begins at the end of the story. It only shows what you have accomplished—not how you did it.

Scene 1: _____
_____
_____

Scene 2: _____
_____
_____

Scene 3: _____
_____
_____

Scene 4: _____
_____
_____

© 1988, THE IMAGINATION STORE, 2424 BEEKMAN ST., CINCINNATI, OH 45214

## TECHNIQUE #6

1. In IMAGIVISION, the movie begins at the end of the story.
2. The Imagivision Movie shows only what you have accomplished—not how you did it.

**WARNING**

IF THIS TECHNIQUE IS NOT USED PROP-
ERLY; IF YOU ATTEMPT TO OVERPOWER
OTHER PEOPLE IN ORDER TO ATTAIN
YOUR DESIRE, YOU WILL HAVE TO REC-
TIFY THE WRONGS YOU HAVE DONE
MANY TIMES OVER. LET YOUR CON-
SCIENCE BE YOUR GUIDE.

# SELF-EVALUATION CHECK LIST
# The Mental Mirror™

*"The Rich Get Richer
And The Poor Get Poorer..."*

*The Rich Get Richer Because They See The Abundance
They Already Have, Which Causes Them To Have
More. The Poor Get Poorer Because They See The
Things They Don't Have, Which Causes Them To
Have Less.*

_____*USING ALL THREE PARTS*

Before using the Self-Evaluation Check List, allow me to backtrack a bit to Chapter II, "Understanding Yourself." In it, we discussed the three parts of a human being: Physical, Mental, and Spiritual. Without using all three parts in everything we do, there is little or no chance of getting the things we desire in life. One of the main reasons we don't succeed is because we refuse to use all three parts in unison.

_____*THE PHYSICAL*

Some of us live in a purely Physical world for the most part. We can work eighteen hours a day, seven days a week, grit our teeth and literally "take on the world." The chronicles of history prove that many people have attempted to "conquer" the world only to fail. Isn't it odd how many famous persons are known more by their failures than by their successes? It's true. No one will ever conquer the world. Yet, some still attempt to do so and will continue this folly until the end of time. It obviously follows that by living in the Physical only, success will always elude us.

248 BEYOND THE SUBCONSCIOUS

## THE MENTAL

Intellectually, we can become a walking encyclopedia, memorizing a vast storehouse of information, yet, odds are, we still won't obtain much because, to us, the world becomes logical—man-made logic. Yet, the world itself is not a logical entity since a Higher Force created it and we cannot explain it through logic. All we can do is try our best to accept nature's workings.

## THE SPIRITUAL

The Spiritual part of ourselves is the one we know best. We've been led to believe, however, that we don't know it and cannot understand it; that it's some sort of mysterious part of ourselves, understood by only a "select few." It's only by using the Spiritual part of ourselves, in conjunction with the other two, that we can gain riches beyond our dreams. But first, it's necessary to separate fact from fiction, myth from reality.

## WHAT IS, ISN'T: WHAT ISN'T, IS

Life is certainly full of surprises, isn't it? One day we believe in something, only to find out later it wasn't true. It seems as though we just can't depend or fully rely on the advice or persuasion of others, because, likely as not, they are wrong, misinformed or, to put it bluntly, pompous, self-centered and egotistical. Far too often, we are confronted by these self-made saviors of the world who lead us, like sheep, down the golden path to self-destruction. One merely has to look through a few pages of history to read about these "leaders" of the world who exploited others for personal satisfaction and gain. Nothing has changed; the same people still exist today—only in different guises. The ones who talk the loudest and tell us how to conduct our lives are not telling the truth.

The truth is subtle; the truth doesn't shout or force us to do anything, nor does it judge us. The truth is the truth. We do not need for it to be shouted at us. We do not need to listen to the rantings and ravings uttered by ego-maniacs. We do not need to be told what to do and when to do it. We do not need to be led by the hand to ultimate failure and subservience. All we need is the powerful force that lies within our Spiritual self and listen to the "still small voice" which tells us right from wrong. And we can reach it by going beyond the subconscious and communicating with it through our Imagination. Therein lies the true secret. Remember that the Spiritual part of ourselves is the easiest to understand if only we give it a chance.

## USE ALL THREE PARTS

The answer to anyone's happiness and peace of mind is to use all three parts of ourselves, Physical, Mental and Spiritual, each and every day. How can we achieve this in an organized way? By using some sort of check list. After all, any successful business uses a check list because it's a simple, accurate way to record transactions. Therefore, I have devised a simple-to-use Self-Evaluation Check List which has proved to be an invaluable aid over the years. When used daily, it will give you a good look at yourself and pinpoint areas that need to be improved. It's a "Mental Mirror."

## HOW THE LIST WORKS

As you can see by the examples that follow, the Self-Evaluation Check List contains 20 questions. These are divided into three categories: Physical, Mental and Spiritual.

The Physical part of the check list covers the three basic areas of eating, sleeping and exercise. The Mental segment asks how much knowledge you acquire each day. The Spiritual part, the most important, discusses your desires and the intensity in which you imagined them. By using all three parts of yourself each day, and keeping an accurate record, you condition yourself for success.

## PHYSICAL CHECK LIST

The first question is, "Did I get enough sleep?" Grade yourself from 0 for no sleep, to 5 for an adequate amount. After circling the proper number, ask yourself the second question, "Did I feel alert and rested?" Again, grade yourself from 0 to 5, depending on how you felt during the day.

In response to the third question, "Did I eat right

today?" again grade yourself from 0 to 5. The fourth question asks, "Did I eat enough whole foods today?" By whole foods, I mean nature's foods versus man-made foods. An apple is a whole food but an apple pie is man-made. Grade yourself accordingly for food eaten in its natural, whole state.

The fifth question in the Physical part of the list asks, "Did I get my proper exercise today?" Circle the correct number regardless of the form of exercise. For example, if simple walking appeals to you, then do it daily. In any case, choose the type of exercise that best suits you.

Now, let us discuss the significance of the Physical Check List. Too many of us take sleep for granted, yet, it's vitally important. People who "get by" on one, two or even three hours of sleep a day will, more than likely, be tired a good deal of the time. Make sure you get adequate sleep EVERY day in order to think clearly and stay physically strong.

_____*WE ARE WHAT WE EAT*

Eating well-balanced, well-proportioned meals is such an obvious necessity, yet we all know too well how we gorge ourselves with all sorts of foods that could prove to be injurious to our health. Some of us treat our cars better than our bodies. We'll go out and buy a new car, put the best gas and oil in it, wash and wax it and treat this inanimate object as though it were royalty. At the same time, we proceed to stuff ourselves with such tidbits as tacos, hamburgers, potato chips, candy bars, ice cream, soft drinks, etc. We are what we eat and we must be careful of what we consume, physically, mentally and spiritually. In the Physical sense, eating more whole foods daily can do much to keep our bodies healthy. Fresh vegetables, fruits, nuts and grains are so abundant in nature, yet we continually devise new types of manufactured foods that are full of empty calories. You might be thinking that this advice I'm giving you is so simple and so well-known that it's a waste of print. If this is true then why don't more of us follow it? The truth is, nature again has given us the answer and we continue to ignore it.

_____*MENTAL CHECK LIST*

The performance of today's complex computers is nothing short of amazing. Yet a computer can do nothing until it's fed information. In spite of the awesome knowledge we have acquired during the past century or so, we continue to hunger for new knowledge, further information about our world and the universe that surrounds us. Therefore, it's important for you to increase your knowledge daily. By doing so, you keep your mind sharp and your Imagination open to fresh desires. Grade yourself from 0 to 5 for question six, "Did I Acquire New Knowledge Today?"

_____*SPIRITUAL CHECK LIST*

The Spiritual part of the Self-Evaluation Check List starts out with listing four of your main desires that you imagined for the day. List these desires in the blanks from seven through ten, then grade yourself from 0 to 5 depending on how well you imagined each one. This will act as a constant visual guide and will do much in helping you attain your desires.

The next four questions, eleven through fourteen, ask: "DID I IMAGINE MYSELF—Being Successful; Being Self-Confident; In Perfect Health, and A Happy Person?" Again, grade yourself from 0 to 5 depending on the intensity of your "Imagining."

Question Fifteen asks, "Did I feel 'Pins and Needles' when I imagined?" Be fair to yourself and grade accordingly. Some people feel the "pins and needles" sensation frequently when they communicate through their Imagination; others feel it moderately while still others hardly feel it at all. Whether you do or not to any great extent is not important in achieving your desires, as stated earlier. You'll know it when it happens because it's an automatic physical sensation.

Question Sixteen asks "Did I see, feel, hear, touch, and smell my desires?" It's very important to experience all these sensations because that's what you must do to stimulate your Imagination. These sensations can become so strong while you're communicating with the Higher Force through your Imagination that you can "reach out" and touch your desires!

Question Seventeen is, "Did I repeat positive statements today?" We all know how many times we repeat NEGATIVE statements! All we have to do is listen to our neighbors; at work, on the bus, in the car—anyplace— and all we hear are gripes about everything from the weather to what's going on in politics. Just for a change,

and a dramatic one at that, try some POSITIVE state-
ments. Here are a few samples you might like to try:
"I am created to succeed."
"I am healthy."
"I am successful."
"I am wealthy."
"I am happy."
"I am intelligent."
"I love everything."
"I love everything that ever lived and everything
that is living now, and everything that will live in the
future."

By repeating POSITIVE statements over and over,
instead of NEGATIVE statements, you will achieve a certain sense of perception you never experienced before. You
will gain a fresh new outlook on life. Let's face it, we aren't
going to solve all the world's problems next week, next
month, a year from now—or ever. All we can do is make
the best of things and thank the Higher Force for grant-
ing us what we have! Many of us go around proclaiming
we have nothing. Yet nature, if we allow it, gives us good
health, intelligence and the willpower to better ourselves.
Through our own efforts we have homes in which to live;
indoor plumbing with hot and cold running water; air
conditioning; heat; food to eat; police and fire departments and advance medical facilities, just to name a few.

_____*THANK YOU!*

Many of us don't realize how powerful the two words
"Thank You!" really are. We say them to each other every
day. They are deeply rooted in our minds because they

signify the end of a transaction; cause and effect—thank you! Since we use the expression with our neighbors, then why not use it with the Higher Force from which all our blessings come? If nothing else, it's simply the courteous thing to do. And while we're thanking the Higher Force for the things we already have, let us also give thanks for the things we don't have as yet, but "pretend" we do. We will possess them in the proper amount of time.

_____*A PARADOX:*
**Why The Rich Get Richer And The Poor Get Poorer.**

This might be a little difficult to understand but when you think about it, you'll see the truth it holds. The old saying, "The rich get richer and the poor get poorer," is certainly true. Have you ever wondered why? Simply stated, the rich get richer because they see the abundance they already have which causes them to have more. The poor see the things they don't have and, as a result, they have less. They spend most of their time complaining but do nothing to alleviate the situation. Either way, it's impossible to count everything we have just as it's impossible to count the things we don't have. Thank the Higher Force for the things you have and the things you will have in the future and you will prosper. Complain about the things you don't have and you will fail. Have you ever seen a happy person who chronically complains? How would you judge yourself?

Question Eighteen is: "Did I Project Love And Compassion To All Mankind?" Again, circle from 0 to 5 according to how you felt. Sometimes it's difficult to pinpoint circumstances in which you feel love and compassion for all mankind. Yet, you can experience this sensation in subtle ways, some of which you may not be aware when they happen. Here are five that can happen every day:

- Pay someone an honest compliment.
- Smile at things that please you during the day.
- Give someone an encouraging word or two.
- Be understanding to someone's plight.
- Listen to others instead of talking about your own viewpoints.

There are many other ways you can feel love and compassion. Be on the lookout for opportunities and you will find them. In this way you will become a better person and be more receptive to receiving your desires.

## COUNT YOUR BLESSINGS

Question Nineteen asks, "Did I Count My Blessings Today?" Before grading yourself from 0 to 5, read the following carefully:

Instead of constantly complaining about things like the rent, mortgage payments, gas and electric bills, cost of food and a myriad of other services and products, we should be thanking the Higher Force within us for the things we do have. Then we should thank the Higher Force for the things we don't have as yet, but desire, and we shall receive them. If we thank the Higher Force for the things we have now and for the things we shall receive in the future, we will prosper beyond expectations and our blessings will be endless.

Right at this moment, our blessings surround us in a protective society for which we should be thankful. During the past century, science has made more strides than in any other period of history. It would be impossible to list all the blessings we have today; there are literally thousands upon thousands and we receive new ones constantly. Following is just a smattering of the blessings we take for granted, day in and day out. Look them over then add a few of your own. You'll soon realize their magnitude and more fully appreciate the things we have now and those things which already exist in the future.

_____*THE LIST OF BLESSINGS*

- Three nutritious, hot meals a day.
- A warm, comfortable bed to sleep in.
- Neat, functional homes in which to live.
- Free libraries containing the knowledge of the world and universe.
- Heat, electricity and air conditioning to cool and warm us at will.
- Giant processing plants to clean the water we drink and supply the power to light our cities and homes.
- Inside plumbing with hot and cold water to cleanse our bodies.
- Police departments to protect us from harm.
- Fire departments to save our property.

- Life insurance to protect our loved ones from financial chaos.

- Doctors, nurses and dentists to save our lives; keep us healthy and help us live longer.

- Large hospitals with modern facilities and the means to cure the diseases of mankind.

- Free schools for those who desire good educations so that they may better themselves and be prepared for the future.

- Supermarkets and shopping malls to bring us exotic foods and goods from all over the world.

- Social Security to augment our incomes in our golden years.

- Counseling and care for the aged so they might have a happier life filled with productivity and usefulness to society.

- Freedom of speech guaranteed by the Constitution and Bill of Rights, including the right to assemble and vote.

- A Republic in which all men are created equal, with liberty and justice for all.

- Free enterprise in which anyone can participate and prosper in direct ratio to the amount of effort put into it.

- A Supreme Court which, to the best of its ability, guarantees justice to every individual.

- Lawyers to defend the innocent and help convict the guilty.

- Vast highways which span the nation and bring our

great cities closer together so that we may better understand each other and create a still better environment.

- Space technology that brings the universe within our range so that someday we will have a better grasp as to the meaning of our existence.

- Pastors, priests, nuns, rabbis, ministers, missionaries and others who devote their lives to caring for the religious needs of all who ask for their guidance and counseling.

- Entertainment of all sorts, including radio, television, movies, theatres, sports, games, parks, recreation, etc.

- Armed Forces to protect our country.

- Museums containing the greatest art from all over the world, spanning centuries from ancient Greece to modern America.

- Cars, buses, planes and trains to take us anywhere we wish to go.

- The capability to love our fellow man, love ourselves and love the Higher Force which gives us our blessings— now—and in the future. **With this love we have HOPE for a world at peace.**

_____*WHAT ARE YOUR SPECIAL BLESSINGS?*

- _____
- _____
- _____
- _____
- _____

- _____
- _____
- _____

## NOW, GRADE YOURSELF
## FROM 0 TO 5 FOR QUESTION #19.

_____*HOW TO GRADE YOURSELF*

The final question, number twenty, asks, "How Was My Day?" Before you circle the letter symbol, P, M, F, S, G or E,* join the 19 numbers you have circled in one unbroken line, like Connect-A-Dots. (See sample.) By doing this, you are making a visual connection of all three parts of yourself—Physical, Mental and Spiritual. It's a "Mental Mirror" and gives a profile of yourself for the day.

After you have connected all your numbers in one unbroken line, you are now ready to circle the proper letter symbol which indicates how you felt your day to be, overall.

* If you have a lot of 0's, then circle the "P" which means you had a Poor day. A lot of 1's indicate a Mediocre day while many 2's mean your day was Fair. If you have quite a few 3's your day has been Satisfactory and many 4's will tell you that you had a Good day. Your ultimate goal, of course, is to connect all the 5's in a straight line and circle the letter "E" because that's a sign of Excellence.

Your final step in completing the check list is to write in the numbers of the questions that need improvement. Do this in the space which states: "I Need To Improve #'s: _____."

Don't be discouraged if your graph doesn't improve

dramatically the first week or two. It takes time to change our daily habits and the list is merely there to help us remember the things we should be doing. The important thing is to actually take the few minutes each day to construct your graph. In addition, make sure you are honest with yourself, otherwise you are wasting your time. It's like cheating on a diet or a golf game. You are merely cheating yourself. Personally, I have never scored a perfect graph, with the line going straight down through all nineteen 5's. Frankly, I don't think I, or anyone else, will ever **honestly** attain this. Why? Because no one is perfect.

The true meaning of life is the struggle to better ourselves; to overcome obstacles and to always have a higher mountain to climb; a puzzle to solve and to discover another clue as we attempt to unravel the mysteries of ourselves.

_____*DAILY SELF-EVALUATION CHECK LIST*

## EXAMPLE

**"The Mental Mirror"™**

Day Of Week: Fri._____ Date: _Sept._____ 19??_____

**Physical**

1. Did I Get Enough Sleep?                                  0①2 3 4 5
2. Did I Feel Alert And Rested?                             ⓪1 2 3 4 5
3. Did I Eat Right Today?                                   0 1②3 4 5
4. Did I Eat Enough Whole Foods Today?                      0①2 3 4 5
5. Did I Get My Proper Exercise Today?                      0①2 3 4 5

**Mental**

6. Did I Acquire New Knowledge Today?                       0 1②3 4 5

**Spiritual            DESIRES**

7. Did I Imagine My 1st: _New House_____ Today?        0 1 2③4 5
8. Did I Imagine My 2nd: _Visit Hawaii_____ Today?     0 1 2③4 5
9. Did I Imagine My 3rd: _Meet new mate_____ Today?    0①2 3 4 5
10. Did I Imagine My 4th: _Get better job_____ Today?  0①2 3 4 5
11. Did I Imagine Myself Being Successful?                  0①2 3 4 5
12. Did I Imagine Myself Being Self-Confident?             ⓪1 2 3 4 5
13. Did I Imagine Myself Being In Perfect Health?           0①2 3 4 5
14. Did I Imagine Myself Being A Happy Person?             ⓪1 2 3 4 5
15. Did I Feel Pins And Needles When I Imagined?            0 1②3 4 5
16. Did I See, Feel, Hear, Touch And
    Smell My Desires?                                       0①2 3 4 5
17. Did I Repeat Positive Statements Today?                 0 1 2③4 5
18. Did I Project Love And Compassion
    To All Mankind?                                         0 1 2 3④5
19. Did I Count My Blessings Today?                         0 1②3 4 5
20. HOW WAS MY DAY?
(I Need To Improve #s_1-2-3-4-5-6-9-10-11-12-13-14-15-16-19_) P(M)F S G E

P-Poor    M-Mediocre    F-Fair    S-Satisfactory    G-Good    E-Excellent

After circling the appropriate numbers, connect them from top to bottom
in one unbroken line to determine your graph. Circle the proper letter
which indicates what kind of day you had.

_____DAILY SELF-EVALUATION CHECK LIST

# EXAMPLE

## "The Mental Mirror"™

Day Of Week: <u>Tues.</u>_____ Date: <u>Aug. 5</u>_____ 19<u>??</u>

**Physical**

| | |
|---|---|
| 1. Did I Get Enough Sleep? | 0 1 2③4 5 |
| 2. Did I Feel Alert And Rested? | 0 1 2③4 5 |
| 3. Did I Eat Right Today? | 0 1②3 4 5 |
| 4. Did I Eat Enough Whole Foods Today? | 0 1②3 4 5 |
| 5. Did I Get My Proper Exercise Today? | 0 1 2③4 5 |

**Mental**

| | |
|---|---|
| 6. Did I Acquire New Knowledge Today? | 0 1 2③4 5 |

**Spiritual**             **DESIRES**

| | |
|---|---|
| 7. Did I Imagine My 1st: <u>$75,000</u> Today? | 0 1 2 3④5 |
| 8. Did I Imagine My 2nd: <u>Pay raise</u> Today? | 0 1 2 3④5 |
| 9. Did I Imagine My 3rd: <u>Newer car</u> Today? | 0 1 2③4 5 |
| 10. Did I Imagine My 4th: <u>Lose weight</u> Today? | 0 1 2③4 5 |
| 11. Did I Imagine Myself Being Successful? | 0 1 2 3 4⑤ |
| 12. Did I Imagine Myself Being Self-Confident? | 0 1 2③4 5 |
| 13. Did I Imagine Myself Being In Perfect Health? | 0 1②3 4 5 |
| 14. Did I Imagine Myself Being A Happy Person? | 0 1②3 4 5 |
| 15. Did I Feel Pins And Needles When I Imagined? | 0 1 2 3④5 |
| 16. Did I See, Feel, Hear, Touch And Smell My Desires? | 0 1 2③4 5 |
| 17. Did I Repeat Positive Statements Today? | 0 1 2③4 5 |
| 18. Did I Project Love And Compassion To All Mankind? | 0 1②3 4 5 |
| 19. Did I Count My Blessings Today? | 0①2 3 4 5 |

20. HOW WAS MY DAY?

(I Need To Improve #s  <u>3-4-13-14-18-19</u>  )         P M F⑤G E

P-Poor   M-Mediocre   F-Fair   S-Satisfactory   G-Good   E-Excellent

After circling the appropriate numbers, connect them from top to bottom in one unbroken line to determine your graph. Circle the proper letter which indicates what kind of day you had.

_____*DAILY SELF-EVALUATION CHECK LIST*

## EXAMPLE

### "The Mental Mirror"™

Day Of Week: Fri._____ Date: July 24_____ 19??_____

**Physical**

1. Did I Get Enough Sleep?                    0 1 2 3 4 ⑤
2. Did I Feel Alert And Rested?               0 1 2 3 ④ 5
3. Did I Eat Right Today?                      0 ① 2 3 4 5
4. Did I Eat Enough Whole Foods Today?        ⓪ 1 2 3 4 5
5. Did I Get My Proper Exercise Today?        0 1 2 ③ 4 5

**Mental**

6. Did I Acquire New Knowledge Today?         0 1 2 ③ 4 5

**Spiritual**          **DESIRES**

7. Did I Imagine My 1st: _Ice skating_____ Today?   0 1 2 3 ④ 5
8. Did I Imagine My 2nd: _Public speaking____ Today?   0 1 2 ③ 4 5
9. Did I Imagine My 3rd: _New friends_____ Today?   0 1 2 3 4 ⑤
10. Did I Imagine My 4th: _Public office____ Today?   0 1 2 3 ④ 5
11. Did I Imagine Myself Being Successful?        0 1 2 ③ 4 5
12. Did I Imagine Myself Being Self-Confident?    0 1 2 3 ④ 5
13. Did I Imagine Myself Being In Perfect Health?  0 ① 2 3 4 5
14. Did I Imagine Myself Being A Happy Person?    0 ① 2 3 4 5
15. Did I Feel Pins And Needles When I Imagined?  0 1 2 ③ 4 5
16. Did I See, Feel, Hear, Touch And
    Smell My Desires?                            0 1 2 ③ 4 5
17. Did I Repeat Positive Statements Today?      0 1 2 3 4 ⑤
18. Did I Project Love And Compassion
    To All Mankind?                              0 1 ② 3 4 5
19. Did I Count My Blessings Today?              ⓪ 1 2 3 4 5
20. HOW WAS MY DAY?
(I Need To Improve #s  _3-4-13-14-18-19_ )       P M F ⑤ G E

P-Poor   M-Mediocre   F-Fair   S-Satisfactory   G-Good   E-Excellent

After circling the appropriate numbers, connect them from top to bottom
in one unbroken line to determine your graph. Circle the proper letter
which indicates what kind of day you had.

© 1988, THE IMAGINATION STORE, 2424 BEEKMAN ST., CINCINNATI, OH 45214

## _____DAILY SELF-EVALUATION CHECK LIST

### "The Mental Mirror"™

Day Of Week: _____ Date: _____ 19_____

**Physical**

| | |
|---|---|
| 1. Did I Get Enough Sleep? | 0 1 2 3 4 5 |
| 2. Did I Feel Alert And Rested? | 0 1 2 3 4 5 |
| 3. Did I Eat Right Today? | 0 1 2 3 4 5 |
| 4. Did I Eat Enough Whole Foods Today? | 0 1 2 3 4 5 |
| 5. Did I Get My Proper Exercise Today? | 0 1 2 3 4 5 |

**Mental**

| | |
|---|---|
| 6. Did I Acquire New Knowledge Today? | 0 1 2 3 4 5 |

**Spiritual**          **DESIRES**

| | |
|---|---|
| 7. Did I Imagine My 1st: _____ Today? | 0 1 2 3 4 5 |
| 8. Did I Imagine My 2nd: _____ Today? | 0 1 2 3 4 5 |
| 9. Did I Imagine My 3rd: _____ Today? | 0 1 2 3 4 5 |
| 10. Did I Imagine My 4th: _____ Today? | 0 1 2 3 4 5 |
| 11. Did I Imagine Myself Being Successful? | 0 1 2 3 4 5 |
| 12. Did I Imagine Myself Being Self-Confident? | 0 1 2 3 4 5 |
| 13. Did I Imagine Myself Being In Perfect Health? | 0 1 2 3 4 5 |
| 14. Did I Imagine Myself Being A Happy Person? | 0 1 2 3 4 5 |
| 15. Did I Feel Pins And Needles When I Imagined? | 0 1 2 3 4 5 |
| 16. Did I See, Feel, Hear, Touch And Smell My Desires? | 0 1 2 3 4 5 |
| 17. Did I Repeat Positive Statements Today? | 0 1 2 3 4 5 |
| 18. Did I Project Love And Compassion To All Mankind? | 0 1 2 3 4 5 |
| 19. Did I Count My Blessings Today? | 0 1 2 3 4 5 |
| 20. HOW WAS MY DAY? (I Need To Improve #s_____) | P M F S G E |

P-Poor   M-Mediocre   F-Fair   S-Satisfactory   G-Good   E-Excellent

After circling the appropriate numbers, connect them from top to bottom in one unbroken line to determine your graph. Circle the proper letter which indicates what kind of day you had.

_____*DAILY SELF-EVALUATION CHECK LIST*

**"The Mental Mirror"**™

Day Of Week: _____ Date: _____ 19_____

**Physical**

| | |
|---|---|
| 1. Did I Get Enough Sleep? | 0 1 2 3 4 5 |
| 2. Did I Feel Alert And Rested? | 0 1 2 3 4 5 |
| 3. Did I Eat Right Today? | 0 1 2 3 4 5 |
| 4. Did I Eat Enough Whole Foods Today? | 0 1 2 3 4 5 |
| 5. Did I Get My Proper Exercise Today? | 0 1 2 3 4 5 |

**Mental**

| | |
|---|---|
| 6. Did I Acquire New Knowledge Today? | 0 1 2 3 4 5 |

**Spiritual**            **DESIRES**

| | |
|---|---|
| 7. Did I Imagine My 1st: _____ Today? | 0 1 2 3 4 5 |
| 8. Did I Imagine My 2nd: _____ Today? | 0 1 2 3 4 5 |
| 9. Did I Imagine My 3rd: _____ Today? | 0 1 2 3 4 5 |
| 10. Did I Imagine My 4th: _____ Today? | 0 1 2 3 4 5 |
| 11. Did I Imagine Myself Being Successful? | 0 1 2 3 4 5 |
| 12. Did I Imagine Myself Being Self-Confident? | 0 1 2 3 4 5 |
| 13. Did I Imagine Myself Being In Perfect Health? | 0 1 2 3 4 5 |
| 14. Did I Imagine Myself Being A Happy Person? | 0 1 2 3 4 5 |
| 15. Did I Feel Pins And Needles When I Imagined? | 0 1 2 3 4 5 |
| 16. Did I See, Feel, Hear, Touch And Smell My Desires? | 0 1 2 3 4 5 |
| 17. Did I Repeat Positive Statements Today? | 0 1 2 3 4 5 |
| 18. Did I Project Love And Compassion To All Mankind? | 0 1 2 3 4 5 |
| 19. Did I Count My Blessings Today? | 0 1 2 3 4 5 |
| 20. HOW WAS MY DAY? (I Need To Improve #s_____) | P M F S G E |

P-Poor   M-Mediocre   F-Fair   S-Satisfactory   G-Good   E-Excellent

After circling the appropriate numbers, connect them from top to bottom in one unbroken line to determine your graph. Circle the proper letter which indicates what kind of day you had.

## _____ *DAILY SELF-EVALUATION CHECK LIST*

**"The Mental Mirror"**™

Day Of Week: _____ Date: _____ 19_____

**Physical**

| | |
|---|---|
| 1. Did I Get Enough Sleep? | 0 1 2 3 4 5 |
| 2. Did I Feel Alert And Rested? | 0 1 2 3 4 5 |
| 3. Did I Eat Right Today? | 0 1 2 3 4 5 |
| 4. Did I Eat Enough Whole Foods Today? | 0 1 2 3 4 5 |
| 5. Did I Get My Proper Exercise Today? | 0 1 2 3 4 5 |

**Mental**

| | |
|---|---|
| 6. Did I Acquire New Knowledge Today? | 0 1 2 3 4 5 |

**Spiritual**          **DESIRES**

| | |
|---|---|
| 7. Did I Imagine My 1st: _____ Today? | 0 1 2 3 4 5 |
| 8. Did I Imagine My 2nd: _____ Today? | 0 1 2 3 4 5 |
| 9. Did I Imagine My 3rd: _____ Today? | 0 1 2 3 4 5 |
| 10. Did I Imagine My 4th: _____ Today? | 0 1 2 3 4 5 |
| 11. Did I Imagine Myself Being Successful? | 0 1 2 3 4 5 |
| 12. Did I Imagine Myself Being Self-Confident? | 0 1 2 3 4 5 |
| 13. Did I Imagine Myself Being In Perfect Health? | 0 1 2 3 4 5 |
| 14. Did I Imagine Myself Being A Happy Person? | 0 1 2 3 4 5 |
| 15. Did I Feel Pins And Needles When I Imagined? | 0 1 2 3 4 5 |
| 16. Did I See, Feel, Hear, Touch And Smell My Desires? | 0 1 2 3 4 5 |
| 17. Did I Repeat Positive Statements Today? | 0 1 2 3 4 5 |
| 18. Did I Project Love And Compassion To All Mankind? | 0 1 2 3 4 5 |
| 19. Did I Count My Blessings Today? | 0 1 2 3 4 5 |
| 20. HOW WAS MY DAY? (I Need To Improve #s_____) | P M F S G E |

P-Poor   M-Mediocre   F-Fair   S-Satisfactory   G-Good   E-Excellent

After circling the appropriate numbers, connect them from top to bottom in one unbroken line to determine your graph. Circle the proper letter which indicates what kind of day you had.

## _____DAILY SELF-EVALUATION CHECK LIST

**"The Mental Mirror"™**

Day Of Week: _____ Date: _____ 19_____

**Physical**

| | |
|---|---|
| 1. Did I Get Enough Sleep? | 0 1 2 3 4 5 |
| 2. Did I Feel Alert And Rested? | 0 1 2 3 4 5 |
| 3. Did I Eat Right Today? | 0 1 2 3 4 5 |
| 4. Did I Eat Enough Whole Foods Today? | 0 1 2 3 4 5 |
| 5. Did I Get My Proper Exercise Today? | 0 1 2 3 4 5 |

**Mental**

| | |
|---|---|
| 6. Did I Acquire New Knowledge Today? | 0 1 2 3 4 5 |

**Spiritual**          **DESIRES**

| | |
|---|---|
| 7. Did I Imagine My 1st: _____ Today? | 0 1 2 3 4 5 |
| 8. Did I Imagine My 2nd: _____ Today? | 0 1 2 3 4 5 |
| 9. Did I Imagine My 3rd: _____ Today? | 0 1 2 3 4 5 |
| 10. Did I Imagine My 4th: _____ Today? | 0 1 2 3 4 5 |
| 11. Did I Imagine Myself Being Successful? | 0 1 2 3 4 5 |
| 12. Did I Imagine Myself Being Self-Confident? | 0 1 2 3 4 5 |
| 13. Did I Imagine Myself Being In Perfect Health? | 0 1 2 3 4 5 |
| 14. Did I Imagine Myself Being A Happy Person? | 0 1 2 3 4 5 |
| 15. Did I Feel Pins And Needles When I Imagined? | 0 1 2 3 4 5 |
| 16. Did I See, Feel, Hear, Touch And Smell My Desires? | 0 1 2 3 4 5 |
| 17. Did I Repeat Positive Statements Today? | 0 1 2 3 4 5 |
| 18. Did I Project Love And Compassion To All Mankind? | 0 1 2 3 4 5 |
| 19. Did I Count My Blessings Today? | 0 1 2 3 4 5 |
| 20. HOW WAS MY DAY? (I Need To Improve #s_____) | P M F S G E |

P-Poor   M-Mediocre   F-Fair   S-Satisfactory   G-Good   E-Excellent

After circling the appropriate numbers, connect them from top to bottom in one unbroken line to determine your graph. Circle the proper letter which indicates what kind of day you had.

## _____DAILY SELF-EVALUATION CHECK LIST

### "The Mental Mirror"™

Day Of Week: _____  Date: _____ 19_____

**Physical**

| | |
|---|---|
| 1. Did I Get Enough Sleep? | 0 1 2 3 4 5 |
| 2. Did I Feel Alert And Rested? | 0 1 2 3 4 5 |
| 3. Did I Eat Right Today? | 0 1 2 3 4 5 |
| 4. Did I Eat Enough Whole Foods Today? | 0 1 2 3 4 5 |
| 5. Did I Get My Proper Exercise Today? | 0 1 2 3 4 5 |

**Mental**

| | |
|---|---|
| 6. Did I Acquire New Knowledge Today? | 0 1 2 3 4 5 |

**Spiritual**          **DESIRES**

| | |
|---|---|
| 7. Did I Imagine My 1st: _____ Today? | 0 1 2 3 4 5 |
| 8. Did I Imagine My 2nd: _____ Today? | 0 1 2 3 4 5 |
| 9. Did I Imagine My 3rd: _____ Today? | 0 1 2 3 4 5 |
| 10. Did I Imagine My 4th: _____ Today? | 0 1 2 3 4 5 |
| 11. Did I Imagine Myself Being Successful? | 0 1 2 3 4 5 |
| 12. Did I Imagine Myself Being Self-Confident? | 0 1 2 3 4 5 |
| 13. Did I Imagine Myself Being In Perfect Health? | 0 1 2 3 4 5 |
| 14. Did I Imagine Myself Being A Happy Person? | 0 1 2 3 4 5 |
| 15. Did I Feel Pins And Needles When I Imagined? | 0 1 2 3 4 5 |
| 16. Did I See, Feel, Hear, Touch And Smell My Desires? | 0 1 2 3 4 5 |
| 17. Did I Repeat Positive Statements Today? | 0 1 2 3 4 5 |
| 18. Did I Project Love And Compassion To All Mankind? | 0 1 2 3 4 5 |
| 19. Did I Count My Blessings Today? | 0 1 2 3 4 5 |
| 20. HOW WAS MY DAY? (I Need To Improve #s_____) | P M F S G E |

P-Poor   M-Mediocre   F-Fair   S-Satisfactory   G-Good   E-Excellent

After circling the appropriate numbers, connect them from top to bottom in one unbroken line to determine your graph. Circle the proper letter which indicates what kind of day you had.

## _____DAILY SELF-EVALUATION CHECK LIST

**"The Mental Mirror"™**

Day Of Week: _____ Date: _____ 19_____

**Physical**

| | |
|---|---|
| 1. Did I Get Enough Sleep? | 0 1 2 3 4 5 |
| 2. Did I Feel Alert And Rested? | 0 1 2 3 4 5 |
| 3. Did I Eat Right Today? | 0 1 2 3 4 5 |
| 4. Did I Eat Enough Whole Foods Today? | 0 1 2 3 4 5 |
| 5. Did I Get My Proper Exercise Today? | 0 1 2 3 4 5 |

**Mental**

| | |
|---|---|
| 6. Did I Acquire New Knowledge Today? | 0 1 2 3 4 5 |

**Spiritual**          **DESIRES**

| | |
|---|---|
| 7. Did I Imagine My 1st: _____ Today? | 0 1 2 3 4 5 |
| 8. Did I Imagine My 2nd: _____ Today? | 0 1 2 3 4 5 |
| 9. Did I Imagine My 3rd: _____ Today? | 0 1 2 3 4 5 |
| 10. Did I Imagine My 4th: _____ Today? | 0 1 2 3 4 5 |
| 11. Did I Imagine Myself Being Successful? | 0 1 2 3 4 5 |
| 12. Did I Imagine Myself Being Self-Confident? | 0 1 2 3 4 5 |
| 13. Did I Imagine Myself Being In Perfect Health? | 0 1 2 3 4 5 |
| 14. Did I Imagine Myself Being A Happy Person? | 0 1 2 3 4 5 |
| 15. Did I Feel Pins And Needles When I Imagined? | 0 1 2 3 4 5 |
| 16. Did I See, Feel, Hear, Touch And Smell My Desires? | 0 1 2 3 4 5 |
| 17. Did I Repeat Positive Statements Today? | 0 1 2 3 4 5 |
| 18. Did I Project Love And Compassion To All Mankind? | 0 1 2 3 4 5 |
| 19. Did I Count My Blessings Today? | 0 1 2 3 4 5 |
| 20. HOW WAS MY DAY? (I Need To Improve #s_____) | P M F S G E |

P-Poor   M-Mediocre   F-Fair   S-Satisfactory   G-Good   E-Excellent

After circling the appropriate numbers, connect them from top to bottom in one unbroken line to determine your graph. Circle the proper letter which indicates what kind of day you had.

© 1988, THE IMAGINATION STORE, 2424 BEEKMAN ST., CINCINNATI, OH 45214

## _____DAILY SELF-EVALUATION CHECK LIST

**"The Mental Mirror"™**

Day Of Week: _____ Date: _____ 19_____

**Physical**

| | |
|---|---|
| 1. Did I Get Enough Sleep? | 0 1 2 3 4 5 |
| 2. Did I Feel Alert And Rested? | 0 1 2 3 4 5 |
| 3. Did I Eat Right Today? | 0 1 2 3 4 5 |
| 4. Did I Eat Enough Whole Foods Today? | 0 1 2 3 4 5 |
| 5. Did I Get My Proper Exercise Today? | 0 1 2 3 4 5 |

**Mental**

| | |
|---|---|
| 6. Did I Acquire New Knowledge Today? | 0 1 2 3 4 5 |

**Spiritual**          **DESIRES**

| | |
|---|---|
| 7. Did I Imagine My 1st: _____ Today? | 0 1 2 3 4 5 |
| 8. Did I Imagine My 2nd: _____ Today? | 0 1 2 3 4 5 |
| 9. Did I Imagine My 3rd: _____ Today? | 0 1 2 3 4 5 |
| 10. Did I Imagine My 4th: _____ Today? | 0 1 2 3 4 5 |
| 11. Did I Imagine Myself Being Successful? | 0 1 2 3 4 5 |
| 12. Did I Imagine Myself Being Self-Confident? | 0 1 2 3 4 5 |
| 13. Did I Imagine Myself Being In Perfect Health? | 0 1 2 3 4 5 |
| 14. Did I Imagine Myself Being A Happy Person? | 0 1 2 3 4 5 |
| 15. Did I Feel Pins And Needles When I Imagined? | 0 1 2 3 4 5 |
| 16. Did I See, Feel, Hear, Touch And Smell My Desires? | 0 1 2 3 4 5 |
| 17. Did I Repeat Positive Statements Today? | 0 1 2 3 4 5 |
| 18. Did I Project Love And Compassion To All Mankind? | 0 1 2 3 4 5 |
| 19. Did I Count My Blessings Today? | 0 1 2 3 4 5 |
| 20. HOW WAS MY DAY? (I Need To Improve #s_____) | P M F S G E |

P-Poor   M-Mediocre   F-Fair   S-Satisfactory   G-Good   E-Excellent

After circling the appropriate numbers, connect them from top to bottom in one unbroken line to determine your graph. Circle the proper letter which indicates what kind of day you had.

_____*DAILY SELF-EVALUATION CHECK LIST*

**"The Mental Mirror"™**

Day Of Week: _____ Date: _____ 19_____

**Physical**

| | |
|---|---|
| 1. Did I Get Enough Sleep? | 0 1 2 3 4 5 |
| 2. Did I Feel Alert And Rested? | 0 1 2 3 4 5 |
| 3. Did I Eat Right Today? | 0 1 2 3 4 5 |
| 4. Did I Eat Enough Whole Foods Today? | 0 1 2 3 4 5 |
| 5. Did I Get My Proper Exercise Today? | 0 1 2 3 4 5 |

**Mental**

| | |
|---|---|
| 6. Did I Acquire New Knowledge Today? | 0 1 2 3 4 5 |

**Spiritual**          **DESIRES**

| | |
|---|---|
| 7. Did I Imagine My 1st: _____ Today? | 0 1 2 3 4 5 |
| 8. Did I Imagine My 2nd: _____ Today? | 0 1 2 3 4 5 |
| 9. Did I Imagine My 3rd: _____ Today? | 0 1 2 3 4 5 |
| 10. Did I Imagine My 4th: _____ Today? | 0 1 2 3 4 5 |
| 11. Did I Imagine Myself Being Successful? | 0 1 2 3 4 5 |
| 12. Did I Imagine Myself Being Self-Confident? | 0 1 2 3 4 5 |
| 13. Did I Imagine Myself Being In Perfect Health? | 0 1 2 3 4 5 |
| 14. Did I Imagine Myself Being A Happy Person? | 0 1 2 3 4 5 |
| 15. Did I Feel Pins And Needles When I Imagined? | 0 1 2 3 4 5 |
| 16. Did I See, Feel, Hear, Touch And Smell My Desires? | 0 1 2 3 4 5 |
| 17. Did I Repeat Positive Statements Today? | 0 1 2 3 4 5 |
| 18. Did I Project Love And Compassion To All Mankind? | 0 1 2 3 4 5 |
| 19. Did I Count My Blessings Today? | 0 1 2 3 4 5 |
| 20. HOW WAS MY DAY? (I Need To Improve #s_____) | P M F S G E |

P-Poor   M-Mediocre   F-Fair   S-Satisfactory   G-Good   E-Excellent

After circling the appropriate numbers, connect them from top to bottom in one unbroken line to determine your graph. Circle the proper letter which indicates what kind of day you had.

## _____DAILY SELF-EVALUATION CHECK LIST

**"The Mental Mirror"™**

Day Of Week: _____ Date: _____ 19_____

**Physical**

| | |
|---|---|
| 1. Did I Get Enough Sleep? | 0 1 2 3 4 5 |
| 2. Did I Feel Alert And Rested? | 0 1 2 3 4 5 |
| 3. Did I Eat Right Today? | 0 1 2 3 4 5 |
| 4. Did I Eat Enough Whole Foods Today? | 0 1 2 3 4 5 |
| 5. Did I Get My Proper Exercise Today? | 0 1 2 3 4 5 |

**Mental**

| | |
|---|---|
| 6. Did I Acquire New Knowledge Today? | 0 1 2 3 4 5 |

**Spiritual**          **DESIRES**

| | |
|---|---|
| 7. Did I Imagine My 1st: _____ Today? | 0 1 2 3 4 5 |
| 8. Did I Imagine My 2nd: _____ Today? | 0 1 2 3 4 5 |
| 9. Did I Imagine My 3rd: _____ Today? | 0 1 2 3 4 5 |
| 10. Did I Imagine My 4th: _____ Today? | 0 1 2 3 4 5 |
| 11. Did I Imagine Myself Being Successful? | 0 1 2 3 4 5 |
| 12. Did I Imagine Myself Being Self-Confident? | 0 1 2 3 4 5 |
| 13. Did I Imagine Myself Being In Perfect Health? | 0 1 2 3 4 5 |
| 14. Did I Imagine Myself Being A Happy Person? | 0 1 2 3 4 5 |
| 15. Did I Feel Pins And Needles When I Imagined? | 0 1 2 3 4 5 |
| 16. Did I See, Feel, Hear, Touch And Smell My Desires? | 0 1 2 3 4 5 |
| 17. Did I Repeat Positive Statements Today? | 0 1 2 3 4 5 |
| 18. Did I Project Love And Compassion To All Mankind? | 0 1 2 3 4 5 |
| 19. Did I Count My Blessings Today? | 0 1 2 3 4 5 |
| 20. HOW WAS MY DAY? (I Need To Improve #s_____) | P M F S G E |

P-Poor   M-Mediocre   F-Fair   S-Satisfactory   G-Good   E-Excellent

After circling the appropriate numbers, connect them from top to bottom in one unbroken line to determine your graph. Circle the proper letter which indicates what kind of day you had.

## _____DAILY SELF-EVALUATION CHECK LIST

### "The Mental Mirror"™

Day Of Week: _____ Date: _____ 19_____

**Physical**

|  |  |
|---|---|
| 1. Did I Get Enough Sleep? | 0 1 2 3 4 5 |
| 2. Did I Feel Alert And Rested? | 0 1 2 3 4 5 |
| 3. Did I Eat Right Today? | 0 1 2 3 4 5 |
| 4. Did I Eat Enough Whole Foods Today? | 0 1 2 3 4 5 |
| 5. Did I Get My Proper Exercise Today? | 0 1 2 3 4 5 |

**Mental**

|  |  |
|---|---|
| 6. Did I Acquire New Knowledge Today? | 0 1 2 3 4 5 |

**Spiritual**           **DESIRES**

|  |  |
|---|---|
| 7. Did I Imagine My 1st: _____ Today? | 0 1 2 3 4 5 |
| 8. Did I Imagine My 2nd: _____ Today? | 0 1 2 3 4 5 |
| 9. Did I Imagine My 3rd: _____ Today? | 0 1 2 3 4 5 |
| 10. Did I Imagine My 4th: _____ Today? | 0 1 2 3 4 5 |
| 11. Did I Imagine Myself Being Successful? | 0 1 2 3 4 5 |
| 12. Did I Imagine Myself Being Self-Confident? | 0 1 2 3 4 5 |
| 13. Did I Imagine Myself Being In Perfect Health? | 0 1 2 3 4 5 |
| 14. Did I Imagine Myself Being A Happy Person? | 0 1 2 3 4 5 |
| 15. Did I Feel Pins And Needles When I Imagined? | 0 1 2 3 4 5 |
| 16. Did I See, Feel, Hear, Touch And Smell My Desires? | 0 1 2 3 4 5 |
| 17. Did I Repeat Positive Statements Today? | 0 1 2 3 4 5 |
| 18. Did I Project Love And Compassion To All Mankind? | 0 1 2 3 4 5 |
| 19. Did I Count My Blessings Today? | 0 1 2 3 4 5 |
| 20. HOW WAS MY DAY? (I Need To Improve #s_____) | P M F S G E |

P-Poor   M-Mediocre   F-Fair   S-Satisfactory   G-Good   E-Excellent

After circling the appropriate numbers, connect them from top to bottom in one unbroken line to determine your graph. Circle the proper letter which indicates what kind of day you had.

## _____DAILY SELF-EVALUATION CHECK LIST

### "The Mental Mirror"™

Day Of Week: _____ Date: _____ 19_____

**Physical**

| | |
|---|---|
| 1. Did I Get Enough Sleep? | 0 1 2 3 4 5 |
| 2. Did I Feel Alert And Rested? | 0 1 2 3 4 5 |
| 3. Did I Eat Right Today? | 0 1 2 3 4 5 |
| 4. Did I Eat Enough Whole Foods Today? | 0 1 2 3 4 5 |
| 5. Did I Get My Proper Exercise Today? | 0 1 2 3 4 5 |

**Mental**

| | |
|---|---|
| 6. Did I Acquire New Knowledge Today? | 0 1 2 3 4 5 |

**Spiritual**              **DESIRES**

| | |
|---|---|
| 7. Did I Imagine My 1st: _____ Today? | 0 1 2 3 4 5 |
| 8. Did I Imagine My 2nd: _____ Today? | 0 1 2 3 4 5 |
| 9. Did I Imagine My 3rd: _____ Today? | 0 1 2 3 4 5 |
| 10. Did I Imagine My 4th: _____ Today? | 0 1 2 3 4 5 |
| 11. Did I Imagine Myself Being Successful? | 0 1 2 3 4 5 |
| 12. Did I Imagine Myself Being Self-Confident? | 0 1 2 3 4 5 |
| 13. Did I Imagine Myself Being In Perfect Health? | 0 1 2 3 4 5 |
| 14. Did I Imagine Myself Being A Happy Person? | 0 1 2 3 4 5 |
| 15. Did I Feel Pins And Needles When I Imagined? | 0 1 2 3 4 5 |
| 16. Did I See, Feel, Hear, Touch And Smell My Desires? | 0 1 2 3 4 5 |
| 17. Did I Repeat Positive Statements Today? | 0 1 2 3 4 5 |
| 18. Did I Project Love And Compassion To All Mankind? | 0 1 2 3 4 5 |
| 19. Did I Count My Blessings Today? | 0 1 2 3 4 5 |
| 20. HOW WAS MY DAY? (I Need To Improve #s_____) | P M F S G E |

P-Poor    M-Mediocre    F-Fair    S-Satisfactory    G-Good    E-Excellent

After circling the appropriate numbers, connect them from top to bottom in one unbroken line to determine your graph. Circle the proper letter which indicates what kind of day you had.

_____*DAILY SELF-EVALUATION CHECK LIST*

**"The Mental Mirror"**™

Day Of Week: _____ Date: _____ 19_____

**Physical**

| | |
|---|---|
| 1. Did I Get Enough Sleep? | 0 1 2 3 4 5 |
| 2. Did I Feel Alert And Rested? | 0 1 2 3 4 5 |
| 3. Did I Eat Right Today? | 0 1 2 3 4 5 |
| 4. Did I Eat Enough Whole Foods Today? | 0 1 2 3 4 5 |
| 5. Did I Get My Proper Exercise Today? | 0 1 2 3 4 5 |

**Mental**

| | |
|---|---|
| 6. Did I Acquire New Knowledge Today? | 0 1 2 3 4 5 |

**Spiritual**          **DESIRES**

| | |
|---|---|
| 7. Did I Imagine My 1st: _____ Today? | 0 1 2 3 4 5 |
| 8. Did I Imagine My 2nd: _____ Today? | 0 1 2 3 4 5 |
| 9. Did I Imagine My 3rd: _____ Today? | 0 1 2 3 4 5 |
| 10. Did I Imagine My 4th: _____ Today? | 0 1 2 3 4 5 |
| 11. Did I Imagine Myself Being Successful? | 0 1 2 3 4 5 |
| 12. Did I Imagine Myself Being Self-Confident? | 0 1 2 3 4 5 |
| 13. Did I Imagine Myself Being In Perfect Health? | 0 1 2 3 4 5 |
| 14. Did I Imagine Myself Being A Happy Person? | 0 1 2 3 4 5 |
| 15. Did I Feel Pins And Needles When I Imagined? | 0 1 2 3 4 5 |
| 16. Did I See, Feel, Hear, Touch And<br>Smell My Desires? | 0 1 2 3 4 5 |
| 17. Did I Repeat Positive Statements Today? | 0 1 2 3 4 5 |
| 18. Did I Project Love And Compassion<br>To All Mankind? | 0 1 2 3 4 5 |
| 19. Did I Count My Blessings Today? | 0 1 2 3 4 5 |
| 20. HOW WAS MY DAY?<br>(I Need To Improve #s_____) | P M F S G E |

P-Poor    M-Mediocre    F-Fair    S-Satisfactory    G-Good    E-Excellent

After circling the appropriate numbers, connect them from top to bottom
in one unbroken line to determine your graph. Circle the proper letter
which indicates what kind of day you had.

_____*DAILY SELF-EVALUATION CHECK LIST*

**"The Mental Mirror"**™

Day Of Week: _____ Date: _____ 19_____

**Physical**

| | |
|---|---|
| 1. Did I Get Enough Sleep? | 0 1 2 3 4 5 |
| 2. Did I Feel Alert And Rested? | 0 1 2 3 4 5 |
| 3. Did I Eat Right Today? | 0 1 2 3 4 5 |
| 4. Did I Eat Enough Whole Foods Today? | 0 1 2 3 4 5 |
| 5. Did I Get My Proper Exercise Today? | 0 1 2 3 4 5 |

**Mental**

| | |
|---|---|
| 6. Did I Acquire New Knowledge Today? | 0 1 2 3 4 5 |

**Spiritual        DESIRES**

| | |
|---|---|
| 7. Did I Imagine My 1st: _____ Today? | 0 1 2 3 4 5 |
| 8. Did I Imagine My 2nd: _____ Today? | 0 1 2 3 4 5 |
| 9. Did I Imagine My 3rd: _____ Today? | 0 1 2 3 4 5 |
| 10. Did I Imagine My 4th: _____ Today? | 0 1 2 3 4 5 |
| 11. Did I Imagine Myself Being Successful? | 0 1 2 3 4 5 |
| 12. Did I Imagine Myself Being Self-Confident? | 0 1 2 3 4 5 |
| 13. Did I Imagine Myself Being In Perfect Health? | 0 1 2 3 4 5 |
| 14. Did I Imagine Myself Being A Happy Person? | 0 1 2 3 4 5 |
| 15. Did I Feel Pins And Needles When I Imagined? | 0 1 2 3 4 5 |
| 16. Did I See, Feel, Hear, Touch And Smell My Desires? | 0 1 2 3 4 5 |
| 17. Did I Repeat Positive Statements Today? | 0 1 2 3 4 5 |
| 18. Did I Project Love And Compassion To All Mankind? | 0 1 2 3 4 5 |
| 19. Did I Count My Blessings Today? | 0 1 2 3 4 5 |
| 20. HOW WAS MY DAY? (I Need To Improve #s_____) | P M F S G E |

P-Poor    M-Mediocre    F-Fair    S-Satisfactory    G-Good    E-Excellent

After circling the appropriate numbers, connect them from top to bottom in one unbroken line to determine your graph. Circle the proper letter which indicates what kind of day you had.

_____*DAILY SELF-EVALUATION CHECK LIST*

**"The Mental Mirror"™**

Day Of Week: _____ Date: _____ 19_____

**Physical**

| | |
|---|---|
| 1. Did I Get Enough Sleep? | 0 1 2 3 4 5 |
| 2. Did I Feel Alert And Rested? | 0 1 2 3 4 5 |
| 3. Did I Eat Right Today? | 0 1 2 3 4 5 |
| 4. Did I Eat Enough Whole Foods Today? | 0 1 2 3 4 5 |
| 5. Did I Get My Proper Exercise Today? | 0 1 2 3 4 5 |

**Mental**

| | |
|---|---|
| 6. Did I Acquire New Knowledge Today? | 0 1 2 3 4 5 |

**Spiritual**          **DESIRES**

| | |
|---|---|
| 7. Did I Imagine My 1st: _____ Today? | 0 1 2 3 4 5 |
| 8. Did I Imagine My 2nd: _____ Today? | 0 1 2 3 4 5 |
| 9. Did I Imagine My 3rd: _____ Today? | 0 1 2 3 4 5 |
| 10. Did I Imagine My 4th: _____ Today? | 0 1 2 3 4 5 |
| 11. Did I Imagine Myself Being Successful? | 0 1 2 3 4 5 |
| 12. Did I Imagine Myself Being Self-Confident? | 0 1 2 3 4 5 |
| 13. Did I Imagine Myself Being In Perfect Health? | 0 1 2 3 4 5 |
| 14. Did I Imagine Myself Being A Happy Person? | 0 1 2 3 4 5 |
| 15. Did I Feel Pins And Needles When I Imagined? | 0 1 2 3 4 5 |
| 16. Did I See, Feel, Hear, Touch And Smell My Desires? | 0 1 2 3 4 5 |
| 17. Did I Repeat Positive Statements Today? | 0 1 2 3 4 5 |
| 18. Did I Project Love And Compassion To All Mankind? | 0 1 2 3 4 5 |
| 19. Did I Count My Blessings Today? | 0 1 2 3 4 5 |
| 20. HOW WAS MY DAY? (I Need To Improve #s_____) | P M F S G E |

P-Poor   M-Mediocre   F-Fair   S-Satisfactory   G-Good   E-Excellent

After circling the appropriate numbers, connect them from top to bottom in one unbroken line to determine your graph. Circle the proper letter which indicates what kind of day you had.

## _____DAILY SELF-EVALUATION CHECK LIST

**"The Mental Mirror"™**

Day Of Week: _____ Date: _____ 19_____

**Physical**

| | |
|---|---|
| 1. Did I Get Enough Sleep? | 0 1 2 3 4 5 |
| 2. Did I Feel Alert And Rested? | 0 1 2 3 4 5 |
| 3. Did I Eat Right Today? | 0 1 2 3 4 5 |
| 4. Did I Eat Enough Whole Foods Today? | 0 1 2 3 4 5 |
| 5. Did I Get My Proper Exercise Today? | 0 1 2 3 4 5 |

**Mental**

| | |
|---|---|
| 6. Did I Acquire New Knowledge Today? | 0 1 2 3 4 5 |

**Spiritual**            **DESIRES**

| | |
|---|---|
| 7. Did I Imagine My 1st: _____ Today? | 0 1 2 3 4 5 |
| 8. Did I Imagine My 2nd: _____ Today? | 0 1 2 3 4 5 |
| 9. Did I Imagine My 3rd: _____ Today? | 0 1 2 3 4 5 |
| 10. Did I Imagine My 4th: _____ Today? | 0 1 2 3 4 5 |
| 11. Did I Imagine Myself Being Successful? | 0 1 2 3 4 5 |
| 12. Did I Imagine Myself Being Self-Confident? | 0 1 2 3 4 5 |
| 13. Did I Imagine Myself Being In Perfect Health? | 0 1 2 3 4 5 |
| 14. Did I Imagine Myself Being A Happy Person? | 0 1 2 3 4 5 |
| 15. Did I Feel Pins And Needles When I Imagined? | 0 1 2 3 4 5 |
| 16. Did I See, Feel, Hear, Touch And Smell My Desires? | 0 1 2 3 4 5 |
| 17. Did I Repeat Positive Statements Today? | 0 1 2 3 4 5 |
| 18. Did I Project Love And Compassion To All Mankind? | 0 1 2 3 4 5 |
| 19. Did I Count My Blessings Today? | 0 1 2 3 4 5 |
| 20. HOW WAS MY DAY? (I Need To Improve #s_____) | P M F S G E |

P-Poor   M-Mediocre   F-Fair   S-Satisfactory   G-Good   E-Excellent

After circling the appropriate numbers, connect them from top to bottom in one unbroken line to determine your graph. Circle the proper letter which indicates what kind of day you had.

## _____DAILY SELF-EVALUATION CHECK LIST

### "The Mental Mirror"™

Day Of Week: _____ Date: _____ 19_____

**Physical**

| | |
|---|---|
| 1. Did I Get Enough Sleep? | 0 1 2 3 4 5 |
| 2. Did I Feel Alert And Rested? | 0 1 2 3 4 5 |
| 3. Did I Eat Right Today? | 0 1 2 3 4 5 |
| 4. Did I Eat Enough Whole Foods Today? | 0 1 2 3 4 5 |
| 5. Did I Get My Proper Exercise Today? | 0 1 2 3 4 5 |

**Mental**

| | |
|---|---|
| 6. Did I Acquire New Knowledge Today? | 0 1 2 3 4 5 |

**Spiritual**          **DESIRES**

| | |
|---|---|
| 7. Did I Imagine My 1st: _____ Today? | 0 1 2 3 4 5 |
| 8. Did I Imagine My 2nd: _____ Today? | 0 1 2 3 4 5 |
| 9. Did I Imagine My 3rd: _____ Today? | 0 1 2 3 4 5 |
| 10. Did I Imagine My 4th: _____ Today? | 0 1 2 3 4 5 |
| 11. Did I Imagine Myself Being Successful? | 0 1 2 3 4 5 |
| 12. Did I Imagine Myself Being Self-Confident? | 0 1 2 3 4 5 |
| 13. Did I Imagine Myself Being In Perfect Health? | 0 1 2 3 4 5 |
| 14. Did I Imagine Myself Being A Happy Person? | 0 1 2 3 4 5 |
| 15. Did I Feel Pins And Needles When I Imagined? | 0 1 2 3 4 5 |
| 16. Did I See, Feel, Hear, Touch And Smell My Desires? | 0 1 2 3 4 5 |
| 17. Did I Repeat Positive Statements Today? | 0 1 2 3 4 5 |
| 18. Did I Project Love And Compassion To All Mankind? | 0 1 2 3 4 5 |
| 19. Did I Count My Blessings Today? | 0 1 2 3 4 5 |
| 20. HOW WAS MY DAY? (I Need To Improve #s_____) | P M F S G E |

P-Poor    M-Mediocre    F-Fair    S-Satisfactory    G-Good    E-Excellent

After circling the appropriate numbers, connect them from top to bottom in one unbroken line to determine your graph. Circle the proper letter which indicates what kind of day you had.

# _____DAILY SELF-EVALUATION CHECK LIST

## "The Mental Mirror"™

Day Of Week: _____ Date: _____ 19_____

**Physical**

| | |
|---|---|
| 1. Did I Get Enough Sleep? | 0 1 2 3 4 5 |
| 2. Did I Feel Alert And Rested? | 0 1 2 3 4 5 |
| 3. Did I Eat Right Today? | 0 1 2 3 4 5 |
| 4. Did I Eat Enough Whole Foods Today? | 0 1 2 3 4 5 |
| 5. Did I Get My Proper Exercise Today? | 0 1 2 3 4 5 |

**Mental**

| | |
|---|---|
| 6. Did I Acquire New Knowledge Today? | 0 1 2 3 4 5 |

**Spiritual**                    **DESIRES**

| | |
|---|---|
| 7. Did I Imagine My 1st: _____ Today? | 0 1 2 3 4 5 |
| 8. Did I Imagine My 2nd: _____ Today? | 0 1 2 3 4 5 |
| 9. Did I Imagine My 3rd: _____ Today? | 0 1 2 3 4 5 |
| 10. Did I Imagine My 4th: _____ Today? | 0 1 2 3 4 5 |
| 11. Did I Imagine Myself Being Successful? | 0 1 2 3 4 5 |
| 12. Did I Imagine Myself Being Self-Confident? | 0 1 2 3 4 5 |
| 13. Did I Imagine Myself Being In Perfect Health? | 0 1 2 3 4 5 |
| 14. Did I Imagine Myself Being A Happy Person? | 0 1 2 3 4 5 |
| 15. Did I Feel Pins And Needles When I Imagined? | 0 1 2 3 4 5 |
| 16. Did I See, Feel, Hear, Touch And Smell My Desires? | 0 1 2 3 4 5 |
| 17. Did I Repeat Positive Statements Today? | 0 1 2 3 4 5 |
| 18. Did I Project Love And Compassion To All Mankind? | 0 1 2 3 4 5 |
| 19. Did I Count My Blessings Today? | 0 1 2 3 4 5 |
| 20. HOW WAS MY DAY? (I Need To Improve #s_____) | P M F S G E |

P-Poor   M-Mediocre   F-Fair   S-Satisfactory   G-Good   E-Excellent

After circling the appropriate numbers, connect them from top to bottom in one unbroken line to determine your graph. Circle the proper letter which indicates what kind of day you had.

_____*DAILY SELF-EVALUATION CHECK LIST*

**"The Mental Mirror"™**

Day Of Week: _____ Date: _____ 19_____

**Physical**

| | |
|---|---|
| 1. Did I Get Enough Sleep? | 0 1 2 3 4 5 |
| 2. Did I Feel Alert And Rested? | 0 1 2 3 4 5 |
| 3. Did I Eat Right Today? | 0 1 2 3 4 5 |
| 4. Did I Eat Enough Whole Foods Today? | 0 1 2 3 4 5 |
| 5. Did I Get My Proper Exercise Today? | 0 1 2 3 4 5 |

**Mental**

| | |
|---|---|
| 6. Did I Acquire New Knowledge Today? | 0 1 2 3 4 5 |

**Spiritual**          **DESIRES**

| | |
|---|---|
| 7. Did I Imagine My 1st: _____ Today? | 0 1 2 3 4 5 |
| 8. Did I Imagine My 2nd: _____ Today? | 0 1 2 3 4 5 |
| 9. Did I Imagine My 3rd: _____ Today? | 0 1 2 3 4 5 |
| 10. Did I Imagine My 4th: _____ Today? | 0 1 2 3 4 5 |
| 11. Did I Imagine Myself Being Successful? | 0 1 2 3 4 5 |
| 12. Did I Imagine Myself Being Self-Confident? | 0 1 2 3 4 5 |
| 13. Did I Imagine Myself Being In Perfect Health? | 0 1 2 3 4 5 |
| 14. Did I Imagine Myself Being A Happy Person? | 0 1 2 3 4 5 |
| 15. Did I Feel Pins And Needles When I Imagined? | 0 1 2 3 4 5 |
| 16. Did I See, Feel, Hear, Touch And Smell My Desires? | 0 1 2 3 4 5 |
| 17. Did I Repeat Positive Statements Today? | 0 1 2 3 4 5 |
| 18. Did I Project Love And Compassion To All Mankind? | 0 1 2 3 4 5 |
| 19. Did I Count My Blessings Today? | 0 1 2 3 4 5 |
| 20. HOW WAS MY DAY? (I Need To Improve #s_____) | P M F S G E |

P-Poor   M-Mediocre   F-Fair   S-Satisfactory   G-Good   E-Excellent

After circling the appropriate numbers, connect them from top to bottom in one unbroken line to determine your graph. Circle the proper letter which indicates what kind of day you had.

## _____DAILY SELF-EVALUATION CHECK LIST

**"The Mental Mirror"™**

Day Of Week: _____ Date: _____ 19_____

**Physical**

| | |
|---|---|
| 1. Did I Get Enough Sleep? | 0 1 2 3 4 5 |
| 2. Did I Feel Alert And Rested? | 0 1 2 3 4 5 |
| 3. Did I Eat Right Today? | 0 1 2 3 4 5 |
| 4. Did I Eat Enough Whole Foods Today? | 0 1 2 3 4 5 |
| 5. Did I Get My Proper Exercise Today? | 0 1 2 3 4 5 |

**Mental**

| | |
|---|---|
| 6. Did I Acquire New Knowledge Today? | 0 1 2 3 4 5 |

**Spiritual**          **DESIRES**

| | |
|---|---|
| 7. Did I Imagine My 1st: _____ Today? | 0 1 2 3 4 5 |
| 8. Did I Imagine My 2nd: _____ Today? | 0 1 2 3 4 5 |
| 9. Did I Imagine My 3rd: _____ Today? | 0 1 2 3 4 5 |
| 10. Did I Imagine My 4th: _____ Today? | 0 1 2 3 4 5 |
| 11. Did I Imagine Myself Being Successful? | 0 1 2 3 4 5 |
| 12. Did I Imagine Myself Being Self-Confident? | 0 1 2 3 4 5 |
| 13. Did I Imagine Myself Being In Perfect Health? | 0 1 2 3 4 5 |
| 14. Did I Imagine Myself Being A Happy Person? | 0 1 2 3 4 5 |
| 15. Did I Feel Pins And Needles When I Imagined? | 0 1 2 3 4 5 |
| 16. Did I See, Feel, Hear, Touch And Smell My Desires? | 0 1 2 3 4 5 |
| 17. Did I Repeat Positive Statements Today? | 0 1 2 3 4 5 |
| 18. Did I Project Love And Compassion To All Mankind? | 0 1 2 3 4 5 |
| 19. Did I Count My Blessings Today? | 0 1 2 3 4 5 |
| 20. HOW WAS MY DAY? (I Need To Improve #s_____) | P M F S G E |

P-Poor   M-Mediocre   F-Fair   S-Satisfactory   G-Good   E-Excellent

After circling the appropriate numbers, connect them from top to bottom in one unbroken line to determine your graph. Circle the proper letter which indicates what kind of day you had.

## _____DAILY SELF-EVALUATION CHECK LIST

**"The Mental Mirror"™**

Day Of Week: _____ Date: _____ 19_____

### Physical

| | |
|---|---|
| 1. Did I Get Enough Sleep? | 0 1 2 3 4 5 |
| 2. Did I Feel Alert And Rested? | 0 1 2 3 4 5 |
| 3. Did I Eat Right Today? | 0 1 2 3 4 5 |
| 4. Did I Eat Enough Whole Foods Today? | 0 1 2 3 4 5 |
| 5. Did I Get My Proper Exercise Today? | 0 1 2 3 4 5 |

### Mental

| | |
|---|---|
| 6. Did I Acquire New Knowledge Today? | 0 1 2 3 4 5 |

### Spiritual               DESIRES

| | |
|---|---|
| 7. Did I Imagine My 1st: _____ Today? | 0 1 2 3 4 5 |
| 8. Did I Imagine My 2nd: _____ Today? | 0 1 2 3 4 5 |
| 9. Did I Imagine My 3rd: _____ Today? | 0 1 2 3 4 5 |
| 10. Did I Imagine My 4th: _____ Today? | 0 1 2 3 4 5 |
| 11. Did I Imagine Myself Being Successful? | 0 1 2 3 4 5 |
| 12. Did I Imagine Myself Being Self-Confident? | 0 1 2 3 4 5 |
| 13. Did I Imagine Myself Being In Perfect Health? | 0 1 2 3 4 5 |
| 14. Did I Imagine Myself Being A Happy Person? | 0 1 2 3 4 5 |
| 15. Did I Feel Pins And Needles When I Imagined? | 0 1 2 3 4 5 |
| 16. Did I See, Feel, Hear, Touch And Smell My Desires? | 0 1 2 3 4 5 |
| 17. Did I Repeat Positive Statements Today? | 0 1 2 3 4 5 |
| 18. Did I Project Love And Compassion To All Mankind? | 0 1 2 3 4 5 |
| 19. Did I Count My Blessings Today? | 0 1 2 3 4 5 |
| 20. HOW WAS MY DAY? (I Need To Improve #s_____) | P M F S G E |

P-Poor   M-Mediocre   F-Fair   S-Satisfactory   G-Good   E-Excellent

After circling the appropriate numbers, connect them from top to bottom in one unbroken line to determine your graph. Circle the proper letter which indicates what kind of day you had.

## _____DAILY SELF-EVALUATION CHECK LIST

**"The Mental Mirror"™**

Day Of Week: _____ Date: _____ 19_____

**Physical**

|  |  |
|---|---|
| 1. Did I Get Enough Sleep? | 0 1 2 3 4 5 |
| 2. Did I Feel Alert And Rested? | 0 1 2 3 4 5 |
| 3. Did I Eat Right Today? | 0 1 2 3 4 5 |
| 4. Did I Eat Enough Whole Foods Today? | 0 1 2 3 4 5 |
| 5. Did I Get My Proper Exercise Today? | 0 1 2 3 4 5 |

**Mental**

|  |  |
|---|---|
| 6. Did I Acquire New Knowledge Today? | 0 1 2 3 4 5 |

**Spiritual            DESIRES**

|  |  |
|---|---|
| 7. Did I Imagine My 1st: _____ Today? | 0 1 2 3 4 5 |
| 8. Did I Imagine My 2nd: _____ Today? | 0 1 2 3 4 5 |
| 9. Did I Imagine My 3rd: _____ Today? | 0 1 2 3 4 5 |
| 10. Did I Imagine My 4th: _____ Today? | 0 1 2 3 4 5 |
| 11. Did I Imagine Myself Being Successful? | 0 1 2 3 4 5 |
| 12. Did I Imagine Myself Being Self-Confident? | 0 1 2 3 4 5 |
| 13. Did I Imagine Myself Being In Perfect Health? | 0 1 2 3 4 5 |
| 14. Did I Imagine Myself Being A Happy Person? | 0 1 2 3 4 5 |
| 15. Did I Feel Pins And Needles When I Imagined? | 0 1 2 3 4 5 |
| 16. Did I See, Feel, Hear, Touch And Smell My Desires? | 0 1 2 3 4 5 |
| 17. Did I Repeat Positive Statements Today? | 0 1 2 3 4 5 |
| 18. Did I Project Love And Compassion To All Mankind? | 0 1 2 3 4 5 |
| 19. Did I Count My Blessings Today? | 0 1 2 3 4 5 |
| 20. HOW WAS MY DAY? (I Need To Improve #s_____) | P M F S G E |

P-Poor   M-Mediocre   F-Fair   S-Satisfactory   G-Good   E-Excellent

After circling the appropriate numbers, connect them from top to bottom in one unbroken line to determine your graph. Circle the proper letter which indicates what kind of day you had.

_____*DAILY SELF-EVALUATION CHECK LIST*

**"The Mental Mirror"™**

Day Of Week: _____ Date: _____ 19_____

**Physical**

| | |
|---|---|
| 1. Did I Get Enough Sleep? | 0 1 2 3 4 5 |
| 2. Did I Feel Alert And Rested? | 0 1 2 3 4 5 |
| 3. Did I Eat Right Today? | 0 1 2 3 4 5 |
| 4. Did I Eat Enough Whole Foods Today? | 0 1 2 3 4 5 |
| 5. Did I Get My Proper Exercise Today? | 0 1 2 3 4 5 |

**Mental**

| | |
|---|---|
| 6. Did I Acquire New Knowledge Today? | 0 1 2 3 4 5 |

**Spiritual          DESIRES**

| | |
|---|---|
| 7. Did I Imagine My 1st: _____ Today? | 0 1 2 3 4 5 |
| 8. Did I Imagine My 2nd: _____ Today? | 0 1 2 3 4 5 |
| 9. Did I Imagine My 3rd: _____ Today? | 0 1 2 3 4 5 |
| 10. Did I Imagine My 4th: _____ Today? | 0 1 2 3 4 5 |
| 11. Did I Imagine Myself Being Successful? | 0 1 2 3 4 5 |
| 12. Did I Imagine Myself Being Self-Confident? | 0 1 2 3 4 5 |
| 13. Did I Imagine Myself Being In Perfect Health? | 0 1 2 3 4 5 |
| 14. Did I Imagine Myself Being A Happy Person? | 0 1 2 3 4 5 |
| 15. Did I Feel Pins And Needles When I Imagined? | 0 1 2 3 4 5 |
| 16. Did I See, Feel, Hear, Touch And Smell My Desires? | 0 1 2 3 4 5 |
| 17. Did I Repeat Positive Statements Today? | 0 1 2 3 4 5 |
| 18. Did I Project Love And Compassion To All Mankind? | 0 1 2 3 4 5 |
| 19. Did I Count My Blessings Today? | 0 1 2 3 4 5 |
| 20. HOW WAS MY DAY? (I Need To Improve #s_____) | P M F S G E |

P-Poor   M-Mediocre   F-Fair   S-Satisfactory   G-Good   E-Excellent

After circling the appropriate numbers, connect them from top to bottom in one unbroken line to determine your graph. Circle the proper letter which indicates what kind of day you had.

## _____DAILY SELF-EVALUATION CHECK LIST

### "The Mental Mirror"™

Day Of Week: _____ Date: _____ 19_____

**Physical**

| | |
|---|---|
| 1. Did I Get Enough Sleep? | 0 1 2 3 4 5 |
| 2. Did I Feel Alert And Rested? | 0 1 2 3 4 5 |
| 3. Did I Eat Right Today? | 0 1 2 3 4 5 |
| 4. Did I Eat Enough Whole Foods Today? | 0 1 2 3 4 5 |
| 5. Did I Get My Proper Exercise Today? | 0 1 2 3 4 5 |

**Mental**

| | |
|---|---|
| 6. Did I Acquire New Knowledge Today? | 0 1 2 3 4 5 |

**Spiritual**                **DESIRES**

| | |
|---|---|
| 7. Did I Imagine My 1st: _____ Today? | 0 1 2 3 4 5 |
| 8. Did I Imagine My 2nd: _____ Today? | 0 1 2 3 4 5 |
| 9. Did I Imagine My 3rd: _____ Today? | 0 1 2 3 4 5 |
| 10. Did I Imagine My 4th: _____ Today? | 0 1 2 3 4 5 |
| 11. Did I Imagine Myself Being Successful? | 0 1 2 3 4 5 |
| 12. Did I Imagine Myself Being Self-Confident? | 0 1 2 3 4 5 |
| 13. Did I Imagine Myself Being In Perfect Health? | 0 1 2 3 4 5 |
| 14. Did I Imagine Myself Being A Happy Person? | 0 1 2 3 4 5 |
| 15. Did I Feel Pins And Needles When I Imagined? | 0 1 2 3 4 5 |
| 16. Did I See, Feel, Hear, Touch And Smell My Desires? | 0 1 2 3 4 5 |
| 17. Did I Repeat Positive Statements Today? | 0 1 2 3 4 5 |
| 18. Did I Project Love And Compassion To All Mankind? | 0 1 2 3 4 5 |
| 19. Did I Count My Blessings Today? | 0 1 2 3 4 5 |
| 20. HOW WAS MY DAY? (I Need To Improve #s_____) | P M F S G E |

P-Poor   M-Mediocre   F-Fair   S-Satisfactory   G-Good   E-Excellent

After circling the appropriate numbers, connect them from top to bottom in one unbroken line to determine your graph. Circle the proper letter which indicates what kind of day you had.

## _____DAILY SELF-EVALUATION CHECK LIST_

**"The Mental Mirror"™**

Day Of Week: _____ Date: _____ 19_____

**Physical**

| | |
|---|---|
| 1. Did I Get Enough Sleep? | 0 1 2 3 4 5 |
| 2. Did I Feel Alert And Rested? | 0 1 2 3 4 5 |
| 3. Did I Eat Right Today? | 0 1 2 3 4 5 |
| 4. Did I Eat Enough Whole Foods Today? | 0 1 2 3 4 5 |
| 5. Did I Get My Proper Exercise Today? | 0 1 2 3 4 5 |

**Mental**

| | |
|---|---|
| 6. Did I Acquire New Knowledge Today? | 0 1 2 3 4 5 |

**Spiritual**          **DESIRES**

| | |
|---|---|
| 7. Did I Imagine My 1st: _____ Today? | 0 1 2 3 4 5 |
| 8. Did I Imagine My 2nd: _____ Today? | 0 1 2 3 4 5 |
| 9. Did I Imagine My 3rd: _____ Today? | 0 1 2 3 4 5 |
| 10. Did I Imagine My 4th: _____ Today? | 0 1 2 3 4 5 |
| 11. Did I Imagine Myself Being Successful? | 0 1 2 3 4 5 |
| 12. Did I Imagine Myself Being Self-Confident? | 0 1 2 3 4 5 |
| 13. Did I Imagine Myself Being In Perfect Health? | 0 1 2 3 4 5 |
| 14. Did I Imagine Myself Being A Happy Person? | 0 1 2 3 4 5 |
| 15. Did I Feel Pins And Needles When I Imagined? | 0 1 2 3 4 5 |
| 16. Did I See, Feel, Hear, Touch And Smell My Desires? | 0 1 2 3 4 5 |
| 17. Did I Repeat Positive Statements Today? | 0 1 2 3 4 5 |
| 18. Did I Project Love And Compassion To All Mankind? | 0 1 2 3 4 5 |
| 19. Did I Count My Blessings Today? | 0 1 2 3 4 5 |
| 20. HOW WAS MY DAY? (I Need To Improve #s_____) | P M F S G E |

P-Poor   M-Mediocre   F-Fair   S-Satisfactory   G-Good   E-Excellent

After circling the appropriate numbers, connect them from top to bottom in one unbroken line to determine your graph. Circle the proper letter which indicates what kind of day you had.

## _____DAILY SELF-EVALUATION CHECK LIST

**"The Mental Mirror"™**

Day Of Week: _____ Date: _____ 19_____

**Physical**

1. Did I Get Enough Sleep?                                  0 1 2 3 4 5
2. Did I Feel Alert And Rested?                             0 1 2 3 4 5
3. Did I Eat Right Today?                                   0 1 2 3 4 5
4. Did I Eat Enough Whole Foods Today?                      0 1 2 3 4 5
5. Did I Get My Proper Exercise Today?                      0 1 2 3 4 5

**Mental**
6. Did I Acquire New Knowledge Today?                       0 1 2 3 4 5

**Spiritual**          **DESIRES**
7. Did I Imagine My 1st: _____ Today?    0 1 2 3 4 5
8. Did I Imagine My 2nd: _____ Today?    0 1 2 3 4 5
9. Did I Imagine My 3rd: _____ Today?    0 1 2 3 4 5
10. Did I Imagine My 4th: _____ Today?   0 1 2 3 4 5
11. Did I Imagine Myself Being Successful?                  0 1 2 3 4 5
12. Did I Imagine Myself Being Self-Confident?              0 1 2 3 4 5
13. Did I Imagine Myself Being In Perfect Health?           0 1 2 3 4 5
14. Did I Imagine Myself Being A Happy Person?              0 1 2 3 4 5
15. Did I Feel Pins And Needles When I Imagined?            0 1 2 3 4 5
16. Did I See, Feel, Hear, Touch And
    Smell My Desires?                                       0 1 2 3 4 5
17. Did I Repeat Positive Statements Today?                 0 1 2 3 4 5
18. Did I Project Love And Compassion
    To All Mankind?                                         0 1 2 3 4 5
19. Did I Count My Blessings Today?                         0 1 2 3 4 5
20. HOW WAS MY DAY?
(I Need To Improve #s_____)      P M F S G E

P-Poor   M-Mediocre   F-Fair   S-Satisfactory   G-Good   E-Excellent

After circling the appropriate numbers, connect them from top to bottom
in one unbroken line to determine your graph. Circle the proper letter
which indicates what kind of day you had.

## _____DAILY SELF-EVALUATION CHECK LIST

**"The Mental Mirror"™**

Day Of Week: _____ Date: _____ 19_____

**Physical**

| | |
|---|---|
| 1. Did I Get Enough Sleep? | 0 1 2 3 4 5 |
| 2. Did I Feel Alert And Rested? | 0 1 2 3 4 5 |
| 3. Did I Eat Right Today? | 0 1 2 3 4 5 |
| 4. Did I Eat Enough Whole Foods Today? | 0 1 2 3 4 5 |
| 5. Did I Get My Proper Exercise Today? | 0 1 2 3 4 5 |

**Mental**

| | |
|---|---|
| 6. Did I Acquire New Knowledge Today? | 0 1 2 3 4 5 |

**Spiritual**              **DESIRES**

| | |
|---|---|
| 7. Did I Imagine My 1st: _____ Today? | 0 1 2 3 4 5 |
| 8. Did I Imagine My 2nd: _____ Today? | 0 1 2 3 4 5 |
| 9. Did I Imagine My 3rd: _____ Today? | 0 1 2 3 4 5 |
| 10. Did I Imagine My 4th: _____ Today? | 0 1 2 3 4 5 |
| 11. Did I Imagine Myself Being Successful? | 0 1 2 3 4 5 |
| 12. Did I Imagine Myself Being Self-Confident? | 0 1 2 3 4 5 |
| 13. Did I Imagine Myself Being In Perfect Health? | 0 1 2 3 4 5 |
| 14. Did I Imagine Myself Being A Happy Person? | 0 1 2 3 4 5 |
| 15. Did I Feel Pins And Needles When I Imagined? | 0 1 2 3 4 5 |
| 16. Did I See, Feel, Hear, Touch And<br>Smell My Desires? | 0 1 2 3 4 5 |
| 17. Did I Repeat Positive Statements Today? | 0 1 2 3 4 5 |
| 18. Did I Project Love And Compassion<br>To All Mankind? | 0 1 2 3 4 5 |
| 19. Did I Count My Blessings Today? | 0 1 2 3 4 5 |
| 20. HOW WAS MY DAY?<br>(I Need To Improve #s_____) | P M F S G E |

P-Poor   M-Mediocre   F-Fair   S-Satisfactory   G-Good   E-Excellent

After circling the appropriate numbers, connect them from top to bottom in one unbroken line to determine your graph. Circle the proper letter which indicates what kind of day you had.

## _____DAILY SELF-EVALUATION CHECK LIST

**"The Mental Mirror"™**

Day Of Week: _____  Date: _____ 19_____

**Physical**

| | |
|---|---|
| 1. Did I Get Enough Sleep? | 0 1 2 3 4 5 |
| 2. Did I Feel Alert And Rested? | 0 1 2 3 4 5 |
| 3. Did I Eat Right Today? | 0 1 2 3 4 5 |
| 4. Did I Eat Enough Whole Foods Today? | 0 1 2 3 4 5 |
| 5. Did I Get My Proper Exercise Today? | 0 1 2 3 4 5 |

**Mental**

| | |
|---|---|
| 6. Did I Acquire New Knowledge Today? | 0 1 2 3 4 5 |

**Spiritual**            **DESIRES**

| | |
|---|---|
| 7. Did I Imagine My 1st: _____ Today? | 0 1 2 3 4 5 |
| 8. Did I Imagine My 2nd: _____ Today? | 0 1 2 3 4 5 |
| 9. Did I Imagine My 3rd: _____ Today? | 0 1 2 3 4 5 |
| 10. Did I Imagine My 4th: _____ Today? | 0 1 2 3 4 5 |
| 11. Did I Imagine Myself Being Successful? | 0 1 2 3 4 5 |
| 12. Did I Imagine Myself Being Self-Confident? | 0 1 2 3 4 5 |
| 13. Did I Imagine Myself Being In Perfect Health? | 0 1 2 3 4 5 |
| 14. Did I Imagine Myself Being A Happy Person? | 0 1 2 3 4 5 |
| 15. Did I Feel Pins And Needles When I Imagined? | 0 1 2 3 4 5 |
| 16. Did I See, Feel, Hear, Touch And Smell My Desires? | 0 1 2 3 4 5 |
| 17. Did I Repeat Positive Statements Today? | 0 1 2 3 4 5 |
| 18. Did I Project Love And Compassion To All Mankind? | 0 1 2 3 4 5 |
| 19. Did I Count My Blessings Today? | 0 1 2 3 4 5 |
| 20. HOW WAS MY DAY? (I Need To Improve #s_____) | P M F S G E |

P-Poor    M-Mediocre    F-Fair    S-Satisfactory    G-Good    E-Excellent

After circling the appropriate numbers, connect them from top to bottom in one unbroken line to determine your graph. Circle the proper letter which indicates what kind of day you had.

_____*DAILY SELF-EVALUATION CHECK LIST*

**"The Mental Mirror"**™

Day Of Week: _____ Date: _____ 19_____

**Physical**

1. Did I Get Enough Sleep?                  0 1 2 3 4 5
2. Did I Feel Alert And Rested?             0 1 2 3 4 5
3. Did I Eat Right Today?                   0 1 2 3 4 5
4. Did I Eat Enough Whole Foods Today?    0 1 2 3 4 5
5. Did I Get My Proper Exercise Today?      0 1 2 3 4 5

**Mental**
6. Did I Acquire New Knowledge Today?      0 1 2 3 4 5

**Spiritual**         **DESIRES**
7. Did I Imagine My 1st: _____ Today?    0 1 2 3 4 5
8. Did I Imagine My 2nd: _____ Today?   0 1 2 3 4 5
9. Did I Imagine My 3rd: _____ Today?   0 1 2 3 4 5
10. Did I Imagine My 4th: _____ Today?   0 1 2 3 4 5
11. Did I Imagine Myself Being Successful?      0 1 2 3 4 5
12. Did I Imagine Myself Being Self-Confident?   0 1 2 3 4 5
13. Did I Imagine Myself Being In Perfect Health?   0 1 2 3 4 5
14. Did I Imagine Myself Being A Happy Person?   0 1 2 3 4 5
15. Did I Feel Pins And Needles When I Imagined?   0 1 2 3 4 5
16. Did I See, Feel, Hear, Touch And
    Smell My Desires?                     0 1 2 3 4 5
17. Did I Repeat Positive Statements Today?     0 1 2 3 4 5
18. Did I Project Love And Compassion
    To All Mankind?                      0 1 2 3 4 5
19. Did I Count My Blessings Today?         0 1 2 3 4 5
20. HOW WAS MY DAY?
(I Need To Improve #s_____)    P M F S G E

P-Poor   M-Mediocre   F-Fair   S-Satisfactory   G-Good   E-Excellent

After circling the appropriate numbers, connect them from top to bottom in one unbroken line to determine your graph. Circle the proper letter which indicates what kind of day you had.

# _____DAILY SELF-EVALUATION CHECK LIST

## "The Mental Mirror"™

Day Of Week: _____ Date: _____ 19_____

### Physical

| | | |
|---|---|---|
| 1. Did I Get Enough Sleep? | | 0 1 2 3 4 5 |
| 2. Did I Feel Alert And Rested? | | 0 1 2 3 4 5 |
| 3. Did I Eat Right Today? | | 0 1 2 3 4 5 |
| 4. Did I Eat Enough Whole Foods Today? | | 0 1 2 3 4 5 |
| 5. Did I Get My Proper Exercise Today? | | 0 1 2 3 4 5 |

### Mental

6. Did I Acquire New Knowledge Today?                0 1 2 3 4 5

### Spiritual               DESIRES

| | | |
|---|---|---|
| 7. Did I Imagine My 1st: _____ Today? | 0 1 2 3 4 5 |
| 8. Did I Imagine My 2nd: _____ Today? | 0 1 2 3 4 5 |
| 9. Did I Imagine My 3rd: _____ Today? | 0 1 2 3 4 5 |
| 10. Did I Imagine My 4th: _____ Today? | 0 1 2 3 4 5 |
| 11. Did I Imagine Myself Being Successful? | 0 1 2 3 4 5 |
| 12. Did I Imagine Myself Being Self-Confident? | 0 1 2 3 4 5 |
| 13. Did I Imagine Myself Being In Perfect Health? | 0 1 2 3 4 5 |
| 14. Did I Imagine Myself Being A Happy Person? | 0 1 2 3 4 5 |
| 15. Did I Feel Pins And Needles When I Imagined? | 0 1 2 3 4 5 |
| 16. Did I See, Feel, Hear, Touch And Smell My Desires? | 0 1 2 3 4 5 |
| 17. Did I Repeat Positive Statements Today? | 0 1 2 3 4 5 |
| 18. Did I Project Love And Compassion To All Mankind? | 0 1 2 3 4 5 |
| 19. Did I Count My Blessings Today? | 0 1 2 3 4 5 |
| 20. HOW WAS MY DAY? | |
| (I Need To Improve #s_____) | P M F S G E |

P-Poor   M-Mediocre   F-Fair   S-Satisfactory   G-Good   E-Excellent

After circling the appropriate numbers, connect them from top to bottom in one unbroken line to determine your graph. Circle the proper letter which indicates what kind of day you had.

## _DAILY SELF-EVALUATION CHECK LIST_

**"The Mental Mirror"™**

Day Of Week: _____ Date: _____ 19_____

**Physical**

1. Did I Get Enough Sleep? 0 1 2 3 4 5
2. Did I Feel Alert And Rested? 0 1 2 3 4 5
3. Did I Eat Right Today? 0 1 2 3 4 5
4. Did I Eat Enough Whole Foods Today? 0 1 2 3 4 5
5. Did I Get My Proper Exercise Today? 0 1 2 3 4 5

**Mental**
6. Did I Acquire New Knowledge Today? 0 1 2 3 4 5

**Spiritual**             **DESIRES**
7. Did I Imagine My 1st: _____ Today? 0 1 2 3 4 5
8. Did I Imagine My 2nd: _____ Today? 0 1 2 3 4 5
9. Did I Imagine My 3rd: _____ Today? 0 1 2 3 4 5
10. Did I Imagine My 4th: _____ Today? 0 1 2 3 4 5
11. Did I Imagine Myself Being Successful? 0 1 2 3 4 5
12. Did I Imagine Myself Being Self-Confident? 0 1 2 3 4 5
13. Did I Imagine Myself Being In Perfect Health? 0 1 2 3 4 5
14. Did I Imagine Myself Being A Happy Person? 0 1 2 3 4 5
15. Did I Feel Pins And Needles When I Imagined? 0 1 2 3 4 5
16. Did I See, Feel, Hear, Touch And
Smell My Desires? 0 1 2 3 4 5
17. Did I Repeat Positive Statements Today? 0 1 2 3 4 5
18. Did I Project Love And Compassion
To All Mankind? 0 1 2 3 4 5
19. Did I Count My Blessings Today? 0 1 2 3 4 5
20. HOW WAS MY DAY?
(I Need To Improve #s_____) P M F S G E

P-Poor   M-Mediocre   F-Fair   S-Satisfactory   G-Good   E-Excellent

After circling the appropriate numbers, connect them from top to bottom in one unbroken line to determine your graph. Circle the proper letter which indicates what kind of day you had.

## _____DAILY SELF-EVALUATION CHECK LIST

### "The Mental Mirror"™

Day Of Week: _____ Date: _____ 19_____

**Physical**

| | |
|---|---|
| 1. Did I Get Enough Sleep? | 0 1 2 3 4 5 |
| 2. Did I Feel Alert And Rested? | 0 1 2 3 4 5 |
| 3. Did I Eat Right Today? | 0 1 2 3 4 5 |
| 4. Did I Eat Enough Whole Foods Today? | 0 1 2 3 4 5 |
| 5. Did I Get My Proper Exercise Today? | 0 1 2 3 4 5 |

**Mental**

| | |
|---|---|
| 6. Did I Acquire New Knowledge Today? | 0 1 2 3 4 5 |

**Spiritual**          **DESIRES**

| | |
|---|---|
| 7. Did I Imagine My 1st: _____ Today? | 0 1 2 3 4 5 |
| 8. Did I Imagine My 2nd: _____ Today? | 0 1 2 3 4 5 |
| 9. Did I Imagine My 3rd: _____ Today? | 0 1 2 3 4 5 |
| 10. Did I Imagine My 4th: _____ Today? | 0 1 2 3 4 5 |
| 11. Did I Imagine Myself Being Successful? | 0 1 2 3 4 5 |
| 12. Did I Imagine Myself Being Self-Confident? | 0 1 2 3 4 5 |
| 13. Did I Imagine Myself Being In Perfect Health? | 0 1 2 3 4 5 |
| 14. Did I Imagine Myself Being A Happy Person? | 0 1 2 3 4 5 |
| 15. Did I Feel Pins And Needles When I Imagined? | 0 1 2 3 4 5 |
| 16. Did I See, Feel, Hear, Touch And Smell My Desires? | 0 1 2 3 4 5 |
| 17. Did I Repeat Positive Statements Today? | 0 1 2 3 4 5 |
| 18. Did I Project Love And Compassion To All Mankind? | 0 1 2 3 4 5 |
| 19. Did I Count My Blessings Today? | 0 1 2 3 4 5 |
| 20. HOW WAS MY DAY? (I Need To Improve #s_____) | P M F S G E |

P-Poor   M-Mediocre   F-Fair   S-Satisfactory   G-Good   E-Excellent

After circling the appropriate numbers, connect them from top to bottom in one unbroken line to determine your graph. Circle the proper letter which indicates what kind of day you had.

© 1988, THE IMAGINATION STORE, 2424 BEEKMAN ST., CINCINNATI, OH 45214

## _____DAILY SELF-EVALUATION CHECK LIST

### "The Mental Mirror"™

Day Of Week: _____   Date: _____   19_____

**Physical**

| | |
|---|---|
| 1. Did I Get Enough Sleep? | 0 1 2 3 4 5 |
| 2. Did I Feel Alert And Rested? | 0 1 2 3 4 5 |
| 3. Did I Eat Right Today? | 0 1 2 3 4 5 |
| 4. Did I Eat Enough Whole Foods Today? | 0 1 2 3 4 5 |
| 5. Did I Get My Proper Exercise Today? | 0 1 2 3 4 5 |

**Mental**

| | |
|---|---|
| 6. Did I Acquire New Knowledge Today? | 0 1 2 3 4 5 |

**Spiritual**          **DESIRES**

| | |
|---|---|
| 7. Did I Imagine My 1st: _____ Today? | 0 1 2 3 4 5 |
| 8. Did I Imagine My 2nd: _____ Today? | 0 1 2 3 4 5 |
| 9. Did I Imagine My 3rd: _____ Today? | 0 1 2 3 4 5 |
| 10. Did I Imagine My 4th: _____ Today? | 0 1 2 3 4 5 |
| 11. Did I Imagine Myself Being Successful? | 0 1 2 3 4 5 |
| 12. Did I Imagine Myself Being Self-Confident? | 0 1 2 3 4 5 |
| 13. Did I Imagine Myself Being In Perfect Health? | 0 1 2 3 4 5 |
| 14. Did I Imagine Myself Being A Happy Person? | 0 1 2 3 4 5 |
| 15. Did I Feel Pins And Needles When I Imagined? | 0 1 2 3 4 5 |
| 16. Did I See, Feel, Hear, Touch And Smell My Desires? | 0 1 2 3 4 5 |
| 17. Did I Repeat Positive Statements Today? | 0 1 2 3 4 5 |
| 18. Did I Project Love And Compassion To All Mankind? | 0 1 2 3 4 5 |
| 19. Did I Count My Blessings Today? | 0 1 2 3 4 5 |
| 20. HOW WAS MY DAY? (I Need To Improve #s_____) | P M F S G E |

P-Poor   M-Mediocre   F-Fair   S-Satisfactory   G-Good   E-Excellent

After circling the appropriate numbers, connect them from top to bottom in one unbroken line to determine your graph. Circle the proper letter which indicates what kind of day you had.

## DAILY SELF-EVALUATION CHECK LIST

**"The Mental Mirror"™**

Day Of Week: _____ Date: _____ 19_____

**Physical**

| | |
|---|---|
| 1. Did I Get Enough Sleep? | 0 1 2 3 4 5 |
| 2. Did I Feel Alert And Rested? | 0 1 2 3 4 5 |
| 3. Did I Eat Right Today? | 0 1 2 3 4 5 |
| 4. Did I Eat Enough Whole Foods Today? | 0 1 2 3 4 5 |
| 5. Did I Get My Proper Exercise Today? | 0 1 2 3 4 5 |

**Mental**

| | |
|---|---|
| 6. Did I Acquire New Knowledge Today? | 0 1 2 3 4 5 |

**Spiritual**            **DESIRES**

| | |
|---|---|
| 7. Did I Imagine My 1st: _____ Today? | 0 1 2 3 4 5 |
| 8. Did I Imagine My 2nd: _____ Today? | 0 1 2 3 4 5 |
| 9. Did I Imagine My 3rd: _____ Today? | 0 1 2 3 4 5 |
| 10. Did I Imagine My 4th: _____ Today? | 0 1 2 3 4 5 |
| 11. Did I Imagine Myself Being Successful? | 0 1 2 3 4 5 |
| 12. Did I Imagine Myself Being Self-Confident? | 0 1 2 3 4 5 |
| 13. Did I Imagine Myself Being In Perfect Health? | 0 1 2 3 4 5 |
| 14. Did I Imagine Myself Being A Happy Person? | 0 1 2 3 4 5 |
| 15. Did I Feel Pins And Needles When I Imagined? | 0 1 2 3 4 5 |
| 16. Did I See, Feel, Hear, Touch And Smell My Desires? | 0 1 2 3 4 5 |
| 17. Did I Repeat Positive Statements Today? | 0 1 2 3 4 5 |
| 18. Did I Project Love And Compassion To All Mankind? | 0 1 2 3 4 5 |
| 19. Did I Count My Blessings Today? | 0 1 2 3 4 5 |
| 20. HOW WAS MY DAY? (I Need To Improve #s_____) | P M F S G E |

P-Poor   M-Mediocre   F-Fair   S-Satisfactory   G-Good   E-Excellent

After circling the appropriate numbers, connect them from top to bottom in one unbroken line to determine your graph. Circle the proper letter which indicates what kind of day you had.

_____*DAILY SELF-EVALUATION CHECK LIST*

**"The Mental Mirror"™**

Day Of Week: _____ Date: _____ 19_____

**Physical**

| | |
|---|---|
| 1. Did I Get Enough Sleep? | 0 1 2 3 4 5 |
| 2. Did I Feel Alert And Rested? | 0 1 2 3 4 5 |
| 3. Did I Eat Right Today? | 0 1 2 3 4 5 |
| 4. Did I Eat Enough Whole Foods Today? | 0 1 2 3 4 5 |
| 5. Did I Get My Proper Exercise Today? | 0 1 2 3 4 5 |

**Mental**

| | |
|---|---|
| 6. Did I Acquire New Knowledge Today? | 0 1 2 3 4 5 |

**Spiritual**               **DESIRES**

| | |
|---|---|
| 7. Did I Imagine My 1st: _____ Today? | 0 1 2 3 4 5 |
| 8. Did I Imagine My 2nd: _____ Today? | 0 1 2 3 4 5 |
| 9. Did I Imagine My 3rd: _____ Today? | 0 1 2 3 4 5 |
| 10. Did I Imagine My 4th: _____ Today? | 0 1 2 3 4 5 |
| 11. Did I Imagine Myself Being Successful? | 0 1 2 3 4 5 |
| 12. Did I Imagine Myself Being Self-Confident? | 0 1 2 3 4 5 |
| 13. Did I Imagine Myself Being In Perfect Health? | 0 1 2 3 4 5 |
| 14. Did I Imagine Myself Being A Happy Person? | 0 1 2 3 4 5 |
| 15. Did I Feel Pins And Needles When I Imagined? | 0 1 2 3 4 5 |
| 16. Did I See, Feel, Hear, Touch And Smell My Desires? | 0 1 2 3 4 5 |
| 17. Did I Repeat Positive Statements Today? | 0 1 2 3 4 5 |
| 18. Did I Project Love And Compassion To All Mankind? | 0 1 2 3 4 5 |
| 19. Did I Count My Blessings Today? | 0 1 2 3 4 5 |
| 20. HOW WAS MY DAY? (I Need To Improve #s_____) | P M F S G E |

P-Poor   M-Mediocre   F-Fair   S-Satisfactory   G-Good   E-Excellent

After circling the appropriate numbers, connect them from top to bottom in one unbroken line to determine your graph. Circle the proper letter which indicates what kind of day you had.

_____*DAILY SELF-EVALUATION CHECK LIST*

**"The Mental Mirror"™**

Day Of Week: _____ Date: _____ 19_____

**Physical**

| | |
|---|---|
| 1. Did I Get Enough Sleep? | 0 1 2 3 4 5 |
| 2. Did I Feel Alert And Rested? | 0 1 2 3 4 5 |
| 3. Did I Eat Right Today? | 0 1 2 3 4 5 |
| 4. Did I Eat Enough Whole Foods Today? | 0 1 2 3 4 5 |
| 5. Did I Get My Proper Exercise Today? | 0 1 2 3 4 5 |

**Mental**

| | |
|---|---|
| 6. Did I Acquire New Knowledge Today? | 0 1 2 3 4 5 |

**Spiritual**           **DESIRES**

| | | |
|---|---|---|
| 7. Did I Imagine My 1st: _____ Today? | 0 1 2 3 4 5 |
| 8. Did I Imagine My 2nd: _____ Today? | 0 1 2 3 4 5 |
| 9. Did I Imagine My 3rd: _____ Today? | 0 1 2 3 4 5 |
| 10. Did I Imagine My 4th: _____ Today? | 0 1 2 3 4 5 |
| 11. Did I Imagine Myself Being Successful? | 0 1 2 3 4 5 |
| 12. Did I Imagine Myself Being Self-Confident? | 0 1 2 3 4 5 |
| 13. Did I Imagine Myself Being In Perfect Health? | 0 1 2 3 4 5 |
| 14. Did I Imagine Myself Being A Happy Person? | 0 1 2 3 4 5 |
| 15. Did I Feel Pins And Needles When I Imagined? | 0 1 2 3 4 5 |
| 16. Did I See, Feel, Hear, Touch And | |
| Smell My Desires? | 0 1 2 3 4 5 |
| 17. Did I Repeat Positive Statements Today? | 0 1 2 3 4 5 |
| 18. Did I Project Love And Compassion | |
| To All Mankind? | 0 1 2 3 4 5 |
| 19. Did I Count My Blessings Today? | 0 1 2 3 4 5 |
| 20. HOW WAS MY DAY? | |
| (I Need To Improve #s_____) | P M F S G E |

P-Poor   M-Mediocre   F-Fair   S-Satisfactory   G-Good   E-Excellent

After circling the appropriate numbers, connect them from top to bottom in one unbroken line to determine your graph. Circle the proper letter which indicates what kind of day you had.

_____ _DAILY SELF-EVALUATION CHECK LIST_

**"The Mental Mirror"™**

Day Of Week: _____ Date: _____ 19_____

**Physical**

1. Did I Get Enough Sleep?                          0 1 2 3 4 5
2. Did I Feel Alert And Rested?                     0 1 2 3 4 5
3. Did I Eat Right Today?                           0 1 2 3 4 5
4. Did I Eat Enough Whole Foods Today?              0 1 2 3 4 5
5. Did I Get My Proper Exercise Today?              0 1 2 3 4 5

**Mental**
6. Did I Acquire New Knowledge Today?               0 1 2 3 4 5

**Spiritual**                  **DESIRES**
7. Did I Imagine My 1st: _____ Today?     0 1 2 3 4 5
8. Did I Imagine My 2nd: _____ Today?     0 1 2 3 4 5
9. Did I Imagine My 3rd: _____ Today?     0 1 2 3 4 5
10. Did I Imagine My 4th: _____ Today?    0 1 2 3 4 5
11. Did I Imagine Myself Being Successful?          0 1 2 3 4 5
12. Did I Imagine Myself Being Self-Confident?      0 1 2 3 4 5
13. Did I Imagine Myself Being In Perfect Health?   0 1 2 3 4 5
14. Did I Imagine Myself Being A Happy Person?      0 1 2 3 4 5
15. Did I Feel Pins And Needles When I Imagined?    0 1 2 3 4 5
16. Did I See, Feel, Hear, Touch And
    Smell My Desires?                               0 1 2 3 4 5
17. Did I Repeat Positive Statements Today?         0 1 2 3 4 5
18. Did I Project Love And Compassion
    To All Mankind?                                 0 1 2 3 4 5
19. Did I Count My Blessings Today?                 0 1 2 3 4 5
20. HOW WAS MY DAY?
(I Need To Improve #s_____)              P M F S G E

P-Poor   M-Mediocre   F-Fair   S-Satisfactory   G-Good   E-Excellent

After circling the appropriate numbers, connect them from top to bottom in one unbroken line to determine your graph. Circle the proper letter which indicates what kind of day you had.

© 1988, THE IMAGINATION STORE, 2424 BEEKMAN ST., CINCINNATI, OH 45214

## _DAILY SELF-EVALUATION CHECK LIST_

### "The Mental Mirror"™

Day Of Week: _____ Date: _____ 19_____

**Physical**

1. Did I Get Enough Sleep?                                     0 1 2 3 4 5
2. Did I Feel Alert And Rested?                                0 1 2 3 4 5
3. Did I Eat Right Today?                                      0 1 2 3 4 5
4. Did I Eat Enough Whole Foods Today?                         0 1 2 3 4 5
5. Did I Get My Proper Exercise Today?                         0 1 2 3 4 5

**Mental**

6. Did I Acquire New Knowledge Today?                          0 1 2 3 4 5

**Spiritual**          **DESIRES**

7. Did I Imagine My 1st: _____ Today?    0 1 2 3 4 5
8. Did I Imagine My 2nd: _____ Today?    0 1 2 3 4 5
9. Did I Imagine My 3rd: _____ Today?    0 1 2 3 4 5
10. Did I Imagine My 4th: _____ Today?   0 1 2 3 4 5
11. Did I Imagine Myself Being Successful?                     0 1 2 3 4 5
12. Did I Imagine Myself Being Self-Confident?                 0 1 2 3 4 5
13. Did I Imagine Myself Being In Perfect Health?              0 1 2 3 4 5
14. Did I Imagine Myself Being A Happy Person?                 0 1 2 3 4 5
15. Did I Feel Pins And Needles When I Imagined?               0 1 2 3 4 5
16. Did I See, Feel, Hear, Touch And
    Smell My Desires?                                          0 1 2 3 4 5
17. Did I Repeat Positive Statements Today?                    0 1 2 3 4 5
18. Did I Project Love And Compassion
    To All Mankind?                                            0 1 2 3 4 5
19. Did I Count My Blessings Today?                            0 1 2 3 4 5
20. HOW WAS MY DAY?
(I Need To Improve #s_____ )            P M F S G E

P-Poor   M-Mediocre   F-Fair   S-Satisfactory   G-Good   E-Excellent

After circling the appropriate numbers, connect them from top to bottom in one unbroken line to determine your graph. Circle the proper letter which indicates what kind of day you had.

## _____DAILY SELF-EVALUATION CHECK LIST

**"The Mental Mirror"™**

Day Of Week: _____ Date: _____ 19_____

**Physical**

| | |
|---|---|
| 1. Did I Get Enough Sleep? | 0 1 2 3 4 5 |
| 2. Did I Feel Alert And Rested? | 0 1 2 3 4 5 |
| 3. Did I Eat Right Today? | 0 1 2 3 4 5 |
| 4. Did I Eat Enough Whole Foods Today? | 0 1 2 3 4 5 |
| 5. Did I Get My Proper Exercise Today? | 0 1 2 3 4 5 |

**Mental**

| | |
|---|---|
| 6. Did I Acquire New Knowledge Today? | 0 1 2 3 4 5 |

**Spiritual**          **DESIRES**

| | |
|---|---|
| 7. Did I Imagine My 1st: _____ Today? | 0 1 2 3 4 5 |
| 8. Did I Imagine My 2nd: _____ Today? | 0 1 2 3 4 5 |
| 9. Did I Imagine My 3rd: _____ Today? | 0 1 2 3 4 5 |
| 10. Did I Imagine My 4th: _____ Today? | 0 1 2 3 4 5 |
| 11. Did I Imagine Myself Being Successful? | 0 1 2 3 4 5 |
| 12. Did I Imagine Myself Being Self-Confident? | 0 1 2 3 4 5 |
| 13. Did I Imagine Myself Being In Perfect Health? | 0 1 2 3 4 5 |
| 14. Did I Imagine Myself Being A Happy Person? | 0 1 2 3 4 5 |
| 15. Did I Feel Pins And Needles When I Imagined? | 0 1 2 3 4 5 |
| 16. Did I See, Feel, Hear, Touch And Smell My Desires? | 0 1 2 3 4 5 |
| 17. Did I Repeat Positive Statements Today? | 0 1 2 3 4 5 |
| 18. Did I Project Love And Compassion To All Mankind? | 0 1 2 3 4 5 |
| 19. Did I Count My Blessings Today? | 0 1 2 3 4 5 |
| 20. HOW WAS MY DAY? (I Need To Improve #s_____) | P M F S G E |

P-Poor   M-Mediocre   F-Fair   S-Satisfactory   G-Good   E-Excellent

After circling the appropriate numbers, connect them from top to bottom in one unbroken line to determine your graph. Circle the proper letter which indicates what kind of day you had.

## _____DAILY SELF-EVALUATION CHECK LIST

**"The Mental Mirror"™**

Day Of Week: _____ Date: _____ 19_____

**Physical**

| | |
|---|---|
| 1. Did I Get Enough Sleep? | 0 1 2 3 4 5 |
| 2. Did I Feel Alert And Rested? | 0 1 2 3 4 5 |
| 3. Did I Eat Right Today? | 0 1 2 3 4 5 |
| 4. Did I Eat Enough Whole Foods Today? | 0 1 2 3 4 5 |
| 5. Did I Get My Proper Exercise Today? | 0 1 2 3 4 5 |

**Mental**

| | |
|---|---|
| 6. Did I Acquire New Knowledge Today? | 0 1 2 3 4 5 |

**Spiritual**          **DESIRES**

| | |
|---|---|
| 7. Did I Imagine My 1st: _____ Today? | 0 1 2 3 4 5 |
| 8. Did I Imagine My 2nd: _____ Today? | 0 1 2 3 4 5 |
| 9. Did I Imagine My 3rd: _____ Today? | 0 1 2 3 4 5 |
| 10. Did I Imagine My 4th: _____ Today? | 0 1 2 3 4 5 |
| 11. Did I Imagine Myself Being Successful? | 0 1 2 3 4 5 |
| 12. Did I Imagine Myself Being Self-Confident? | 0 1 2 3 4 5 |
| 13. Did I Imagine Myself Being In Perfect Health? | 0 1 2 3 4 5 |
| 14. Did I Imagine Myself Being A Happy Person? | 0 1 2 3 4 5 |
| 15. Did I Feel Pins And Needles When I Imagined? | 0 1 2 3 4 5 |
| 16. Did I See, Feel, Hear, Touch And Smell My Desires? | 0 1 2 3 4 5 |
| 17. Did I Repeat Positive Statements Today? | 0 1 2 3 4 5 |
| 18. Did I Project Love And Compassion To All Mankind? | 0 1 2 3 4 5 |
| 19. Did I Count My Blessings Today? | 0 1 2 3 4 5 |
| 20. HOW WAS MY DAY? (I Need To Improve #s_____) | P M F S G E |

P-Poor  M-Mediocre  F-Fair  S-Satisfactory  G-Good  E-Excellent

After circling the appropriate numbers, connect them from top to bottom in one unbroken line to determine your graph. Circle the proper letter which indicates what kind of day you had.

© 1988, THE IMAGINATION STORE, 2424 BEEKMAN ST., CINCINNATI, OH 45214

_____DAILY SELF-EVALUATION CHECK LIST

**"The Mental Mirror"™**

Day Of Week: _____ Date: _____ 19_____
**Physical**

| | |
|---|---|
| 1. Did I Get Enough Sleep? | 0 1 2 3 4 5 |
| 2. Did I Feel Alert And Rested? | 0 1 2 3 4 5 |
| 3. Did I Eat Right Today? | 0 1 2 3 4 5 |
| 4. Did I Eat Enough Whole Foods Today? | 0 1 2 3 4 5 |
| 5. Did I Get My Proper Exercise Today? | 0 1 2 3 4 5 |

**Mental**

| | |
|---|---|
| 6. Did I Acquire New Knowledge Today? | 0 1 2 3 4 5 |

**Spiritual              DESIRES**

| | |
|---|---|
| 7. Did I Imagine My 1st: _____ Today? | 0 1 2 3 4 5 |
| 8. Did I Imagine My 2nd: _____ Today? | 0 1 2 3 4 5 |
| 9. Did I Imagine My 3rd: _____ Today? | 0 1 2 3 4 5 |
| 10. Did I Imagine My 4th: _____ Today? | 0 1 2 3 4 5 |
| 11. Did I Imagine Myself Being Successful? | 0 1 2 3 4 5 |
| 12. Did I Imagine Myself Being Self-Confident? | 0 1 2 3 4 5 |
| 13. Did I Imagine Myself Being In Perfect Health? | 0 1 2 3 4 5 |
| 14. Did I Imagine Myself Being A Happy Person? | 0 1 2 3 4 5 |
| 15. Did I Feel Pins And Needles When I Imagined? | 0 1 2 3 4 5 |
| 16. Did I See, Feel, Hear, Touch And Smell My Desires? | 0 1 2 3 4 5 |
| 17. Did I Repeat Positive Statements Today? | 0 1 2 3 4 5 |
| 18. Did I Project Love And Compassion To All Mankind? | 0 1 2 3 4 5 |
| 19. Did I Count My Blessings Today? | 0 1 2 3 4 5 |
| 20. HOW WAS MY DAY? (I Need To Improve #s_____) | P M F S G E |

P-Poor    M-Mediocre    F-Fair    S-Satisfactory    G-Good    E-Excellent

After circling the appropriate numbers, connect them from top to bottom in one unbroken line to determine your graph. Circle the proper letter which indicates what kind of day you had.

## TECHNIQUE #7

1. In achieving our desires, it's vitally important to use all three parts of ourselves: Physical, Mental and Spiritual. We must do this daily.

2. Mankind imparts logic to the world. The world is not a logical entity since it was created by a Higher Force.

3. By existing in a Physical sense only, we cannot possibly succeed. At the same time, we must keep our Physical bodies in the best condition possible.

4. Gain new knowledge each day.

5. By incorporating the Spiritual Self into our daily life, we can attain our desires in the right way—from the Higher Force rather than the Lower Force.

6. Use the Self-Evaluation Check List each day. By doing so, we will be in a better position to attain our desires—at the right time and the right place.

7. High and low grades on the Check List aren't important in themselves. It's using all three parts of ourselves: Physical, Mental and Spiritual, that's paramount to attaining our desires.

# PART THREE

PART THREE

# THE
# ULTIMATE
# ANSWER

*"Anything That Dies
Never Was."*

_____*THE HIGHER FORCE*

Although I have discussed the Higher Force at length in the first two parts of this book, I purposely stayed away from actually "defining" this almighty power for fear it might offend those who adhere to a specific religion or belief, or those whose ego won't permit them to accept the thoughts I'm about to present.

As stated in Chapter Two, the powerful force within us can only be experienced. Learned scholars and theologians have attempted to "explain" this force, this power; however, in my opinion, they have fallen short of its true meaning.

First of all, I feel that this "Force," or whatever other term you wish to use, is the ultimate answer to all our desires. Try as we may we must accept, through our limited perspective, that this is true. We can reach no other conclusion. The problem is, throughout history, OTHERS have told us what to believe concerning the Higher Force and how to believe it. These mortals, born of our own equal, have also dictated what NOT to believe and what not to accept. In my opinion, this knowledge, this inner awareness, has been granted to every individual and no one, I mean NO ONE, should take it upon themselves

312 BEYOND THE SUBCONSCIOUS

to direct our Spiritual lives according to their wishes. We should be the master of our own destinies by allowing the Higher Force to work through us and not be led by wishes of others.

I, like most others, have pondered the mysteries of the universe and the part that I play. I do not pretend to know the inner workings of the Higher Force nor will I attempt to present my thoughts as though they were written in stone. Rather, I have chosen to express my thoughts concerning the Higher Force in a way that will not offend anyone. If you happen to agree with what I have to say, then congratulations. If not, then that is your privilege as a fellow human being. Whether or not you agree, you can be assured that by following the methods and techniques in the first two parts of this book, you WILL get those things you desire.

_____*MY CONCLUSIONS*

After years and years of research, meditation and soul-searching, I have reached certain conclusions regarding the Higher Force. They are hereby presented for your consideration. If nothing else, they will add a little insight into the mystery of life and our purpose in the universe:

_____*ULTIMATE QUESTIONS AND ANSWERS*

QUESTION:  WHAT IS THE HIGHER FORCE?

ANSWER:    I believe the Higher Force is the sum total of everything.

QUESTION: IF THE HIGHER FORCE IS THE SUM TOTAL OF EVERYTHING, WHO ARE WE?

ANSWER: We are either the Higher Force or a part of the Higher Force.

QUESTION: IF WE ARE A PART OF THE HIGHER FORCE, THEN ARE WE A PART OF EACH OTHER?

ANSWER: Yes. If everything is one, then you and I are the same. I am you. You are me. We are ONE.

QUESTION: WHY SHOULD WE LOVE OTHERS AS WE LOVE OURSELVES?

ANSWER: The purpose of life is to believe, to truly KNOW, that the Higher Force is within you. It is the belief that you are now ONE with everything. You are everything— everything is you.

QUESTION: WHO CAN HELP YOU BELIEVE?

ANSWER: Only YOU. It must be done within yourself. Within you dwells the Higher Force.

QUESTION: WHAT HAPPENS WHEN YOU DON'T GO WITHIN YOURSELF AND BECOME ONE WITH EVERYTHING?

ANSWER: The very thing that is happening to you now—you become spiritually dead. What is spiritual death? You become "disconnected" with the Higher Force.

This is the true meaning of "death" because you never really die.

QUESTION:   WHERE DID ALL THIS INFORMATION COME FROM?

ANSWER:   Some of the information came from books; some came from studying nature and some came from people I know. A great amount came from a source that few understand.

Regardless of what we perceive as the Higher Force, we must press on and, eventually, we will find the right combination of insight and knowledge which will elevate our faith and belief to new heights of awareness and understanding.

# <u>CAUTION!</u>
## THIS IS THE LAST RESORT!
## READ ONLY IF ALL ELSE
## HAS FAILED.

**DIRECTIONS: HOLD UP TO MIRROR**

## THE LAST RESORT
THE LAST RESORT

Well, here you are again! You've read this book and what you wanted hasn't happened yet. So, now what are you going to do — quit again? Throw in the towel? Before you do, give yourself one more chance and do the following:

Dry your eyes, grit your teeth and look in the mirror — if you have the courage. The person you see is the most important in the world. If you've been looking for a miracle, one is staring right back at you, for you are a living, breathing miracle.

You must understand that success has been reserved, and is waiting for you — right NOW — if only you don't give up. This is the essential difference between a winner and a loser. Don't sell yourself short. Everything you need for happiness and success is within you — right at this moment.

Tell yourself that you are never going to quit. The reason why you don't get the things you want is because you give up too soon. Now, it's time to take POSITIVE ACTION. Follow the methods and techniques faithfully and don't quit. After all, if you can't take 10—30 minutes a day to improve yourself Physically, Mentally and Spiritually then, perhaps, you don't deserve success! Personally, I think you do. It's up to you.

Eternally Your Friend,
Chuck Francis

_____*THE NEW BEGINNING*

Dear Friend:

I feel as though I have known you forever, and probably have. When you free yourself from your deep spiritual sleep through belief, the world and the universe will be yours for the asking and you will experience love, peace, joy and righteousness.

Eternally Your Friend,

Chuck Francis

320 BEYOND THE SUBCONSCIOUS

# THERE IS NO END

---

## FREE OFFER

Be sure to send for your free copy of our publication, The Imagination Store News, containing informative, inspiring, and motivating articles for physical, mental, and spiritual growth. Send your name and address to:

The Imagination Store
2424 Beekman Street • Department 525
Cincinnati, OH 45214

---